SMART SNACKS

100+ quick & nutritious recipes for surviving the school years

Flip Shelton & Michael Carr-Gregg

mood-
boosting
food for kids
& teens

PENGUIN LIFE

AN IMPRINT OF

PENGUIN BOOKS

The information contained in this book is of a general nature only. If you wish to make use of any dietary information in this book relating to you or your family's health, you should first consider its appropriateness to your/their situation, including consulting a medical professional.

PENGUIN LIFE AUSTRALIA

UK | USA | Canada | Ireland | Australia
India | New Zealand | South Africa | China

Penguin Books is part of the Penguin Random House group of companies whose addresses can be found at global.penguinrandomhouse.com.

Penguin
Random House
Australia

First published by Penguin Random House Australia Pty Ltd 2019

Cover and text design by Adam Laszcuk © Penguin Random House Australia Pty Ltd
Cover and internal photography by Grant Cutelli
Shot at The Bunka, Port Melbourne
Food styling by Leesa O'Reilly
Typeset in Fort by Post Pre-press Group, Queensland, Australia
Colour separation by Splitting Image Colour Studio, Clayton, Victoria
Printed and bound in China by RR Donnelley Asia Printing Solutions Limited

A catalogue record for this
book is available from the
National Library of Australia

ISBN 978 0 14379 253 6

penguin.com.au

CONTENTS

FOREWORD 6

INTRODUCTION 9

HOW TO SNACK WELL 13

HYDRATION 16

TIME (AND COST) SAVING TIPS 19

DEALING WITH THE STRESS OF STUDY 25

1. ON THE BALL 30

2. SMOOTHIES AND JUICES 50

3. DIPS TO DIG INTO 68

4. CHIPS AHOY 86

5. MIDNIGHT MUNCHIES 98

6. FAST FOOD 112

7. COOL THINGS FOR HOT HEADS 122

8. SUPER SANGAS 136

9. ONE BIT WONDERS 146

10. SMART SWEET THINGS 164

ACKNOWLEDGEMENTS 184

FURTHER READING 185

INDEX 187

FOREWORD

Dr Michael Carr-Gregg

I HAVE BEEN A CHILD AND ADOLESCENT PSYCHOLOGIST for more than three decades and there is no doubt that things are not going swimmingly in terms of young people's mental health. The statistics reveal an epidemic of eating disorders, depression, anxiety, self-harm and suicidal ideation which is compromising the health and wellbeing of this generation.

Childhood and adolescence are periods of swift development that are vitally important to developing a sound underpinning for good physical and psychological health later in life. Sadly, almost all the research demonstrates that members of the population I care about most are failing to meet many of the professional recommendations, especially when we examine their diet.

In the 'lucky country', fewer than 5 per cent of teenagers consume the suggested daily amount of fruit and vegetables, and a 2016 study by the Australian Psychological Society found that one in five Australian adolescents consumed soft drinks almost every day or more.[1] With a diet that's commonly high in fat, high in sugar and nutrient poor, it's hardly a surprise that the latest figures reveal that one in four Australian young people are overweight or obese. This ghastly gastronomic situation is backed up by research from Sydney University, published in the *British Journal of Nutrition*, which found especially bad habits in children and adolescents – with a staggering 76 per cent of teenagers exceeding the guidelines for daily sugar intake.[2] Yet despite all the public health campaigns and dietary warnings, during the past two decades there's been basically no reduction in the nation's consumption of sugar.

And while these trends have us headed for the number one spot in the world obesity Olympics, the research is clear that they're impacting on child and adolescent mental health as well. A few years ago, I met Professor Felice Jacka from the Food and Mood Centre at Deakin University, who was studying the relationship between what young people were putting in their mouths and their psychology. I was instantly converted by her scientific rigour and convincing data. Dr Jacka's team has subsequently demonstrated that eating junk foods does indeed increase the likelihood of psychological problems and can also impact on parts of the brain associated with memory and learning.[3] Through her cutting-edge work she has taught me and a generation of psychologists that we need to encourage our clients to adopt a good-quality, healthy diet with plenty of nuts, fruits and vegetables – and that doing so can truly be protective of mental health.

I have long believed that parents need to fight over things that matter: sex, drugs, sleep, curfews, internet use, exercise and, of course, diet. These are issues that relate directly to the wellbeing of our offspring. When I raise the topic of food with my clients, I usually get an eye roll so big that they are in danger of detaching a retina. They are expecting a finger-wagging lecture on the food pyramid and the dangers inherent in a diet of cheap, fast food. And while those dangers are indeed undeniable, Flip and I have written this book not to preach or pass judgement, but to provide parents with a wealth of recipes and ideas for swapping processed snacks and sugary drinks with alternatives that are packed with nourishment, to help tip the balance towards a healthier diet. We've chosen to focus on snacks because they're a key and often overlooked part of kids' food routines. These mini meals are important for maintaining blood sugar levels – with benefits for mood and concentration – but are often where our children reach for sugar or junk food when they could be boosting their nutrition instead. The 'smart snacks' you'll find in the following pages are easy to make, good for mind and body, and – most of all – delicious!

Remember, childhood and the teen years are where many lifetime routines are established. So, if this book can help a generation of Australian families to build healthy lifestyles, and start to educate young people on nutrition, food and cooking, it will arguably be a game changer in adolescent mental health.

INTRODUCTION

Flip Shelton

ONE OF THE MOST EFFECTIVE WAYS to get the best out of your body and brain is with good food. And while there is always a lot of focus on the importance of eating well when it comes to breakfast, lunch and dinner, the snacks in between are just as important, if not more so. The right snacks help to balance blood sugar levels, and therefore moods, more evenly throughout the day. When snacks are well chosen they can keep hunger at bay so we don't arrive at the lunch or dinner table starving hungry and low in energy – the perfect storm for making poor food choices or overeating. However, snacking can go horribly wrong if not enough attention is paid to our choices, which can then derail all the good work of healthy main meals.

What's interesting is that research tells us we're not eating more at the main meal times; rather, the **number** of times we snack each day and the **size** of the snacks we are eating has increased, while the **quality** of the snacks we are choosing is decreasing. Whether you call it oral over-consumption or recreational eating, it's become our favourite pastime.

There are other factors contributing to the rocketing rates of overweight and obese young people, of course, and one of the biggest is the increased amount of time spent on screen-based entertainment such as social media, TV and video games, which results in a drop in physical activity. The *Australia's Health 2016* report discovered that 80 per cent of children and young people aged 5–17 did not meet physical activity recommendations. Nevertheless, you can't out-train a bad diet, which is why it's vital to feed our kids the right things even if they're among the ones who do have an active lifestyle.

Snacks have been very important to me ever since my final years at school when I was studying and noticed the positive power of good food on my mood and blood sugar. Later, when I was training for marathons and Ironman events, I witnessed even more powerfully the impact that food had on me and my training partners. My husband is a coeliac and has competed in more than twenty marathons and numerous Ironman events and ultra-marathons, including the famous Comrades Marathon, an 89 km race in South Africa. Any incorrect food choices have an immediate effect on him and his performance. Then, as a mother, I have seen – and continue to see – how food affects my young son and his friends.

But I'm no robot and I don't believe in eating purely for functionality and fuel – although that does play a big part. I love food. I love looking at it, choosing, cooking and creating it and, of course, savouring it. I've spent my life reading about and experimenting with food: buying cookbooks, writing cookbooks, sharing recipes on the radio and TV, but most importantly asking questions about what's best for us and why.

This book started as a collection of my favourite snacks to keep on file in my own kitchen. They are what I prepare for my family, time and time again. Some have been tweaked and changed over the years and all of them have been taste-tested by kids and adults alike. Many of these recipes have been made in my cooking classes at my son's primary school and now they are here for you and your children to enjoy. What they all have in common is that they're quick and easy to whip up – after all, the best snack is one that's simple!

There are over 100 delicious recipes here that are packed full of protein, complex carbohydrates, essential fatty acids and many different vitamins and minerals.

None of these recipes require scientific or tricky methods so they're perfect for adults and teenagers to make, while younger kids can help out too. Getting the kids involved, whatever their age, not only creates a shared experience but also provides us parents with the opportunity to give them a basic survival skill that will hold them in good stead. What's more, research shows (and experience tells me) that when kids prepare their own food they take ownership of it, which increases the likelihood they will eat it. This is an especially good strategy to use at those times when you want to introduce different ingredients or with kids who are reluctant to try new foods. Get them experimenting in the kitchen and encourage them to sample things along the way. It's amazing how this simple approach eases the pressure and expectations.

There are chapters dedicated to wholefood **smoothies**, perfect for digestion when exam nerves are peaking; icy poles to chill hot heads; **midnight munchies** to calm the body and brain after hours of study; and **fast food** suggestions for hangry kids who have to eat NOW. I'll show you how to make 'happy water' to ensure proper hydration, prepare **smart sweet treats** and rustle up **one bit wonders** at those times when there is seemingly nothing in the fridge or pantry. There are **chips** and **dips to dive into** plus **super sangas** – and you will **have a ball** along the way!

I have used over 80 readily available and familiar ingredients including fruit, veggies, grains and legumes, herbs and spices. There are also ingredients like cacao, maca, lucuma, matcha, hemp seeds and mesquite powder that might seem new but have actually been used in other countries and cultures for years. I hope you'll add these to your shopping list and try them out for the added health benefits they bring. All the snacks are vegetarian, most are gluten-free, and many are paleo- and

FODMAP-friendly. Each recipe is marked according to which dietary box it ticks to make things straightforward.

These days I avoid processed sugar but some of the recipes do include small amounts of raw brown sugar, maple syrup, honey, rice malt syrup or coconut syrup. I use ingredients like vanilla, cinnamon, dates and coconut to give snacks a naturally sweet taste, plus lots of avocados, nuts, seeds and coconut oil for their flavour and good fats to ensure the snack is delicious and creates satiety.

Look out for Michael's tips and nutritional insights that accompany my recipes – he is Australia's leading child and teenage psychologist for good reason, and an absolute fount of knowledge. We sing from the same song book when it comes to the importance of good food, and his contributions will help you discover the impressive range of benefits that these snacks provide. I can't thank Michael enough for bringing his wisdom and wit to these pages.

We both sincerely hope that this book inspires parents and kids to snack smart and proves to be a much-thumbed reference book in home libraries and kitchens around Australia for years to come.

HOW TO SNACK WELL

I'VE FOUND THAT MANY OF US THINK OF SNACKS as inconsequential food eaten randomly (and sometimes even constantly) during the day. Nothing much. A low-cost filler to keep hunger at bay or to satisfy boredom or avoid a task. But seeing them in this way is to our detriment.

Interestingly, the latest research tells us that young people snack when they are happy.[4]

Poor snack choices can unravel us mentally and physically. They can impact our ability to concentrate and quite simply operate anywhere near our optimal level. Eat sugary snacks regularly and you can have more ups and downs than a Frequent Flyer. Eat fried fatty snacks regularly and you can feel as sluggish as a sloth. Eat salty snacks regularly and you can end up as cranky as Blackbeard with an upset tummy and high blood pressure!

So, what is the best way to snack? How should our kids and teens be satisfying their hunger between meals without overeating or disrupting meal patterns?

Here are my top ten tips:

1. **Drink water first.** Keeping fluid levels up is as important as eating well, if not more so – as we'll explain in the following section on hydration (see page 16). A glass of water is always a good place to start.

2. **Eat small, smart snacks often.** When snacks are made with nutrient-dense carbohydrates, healthy fats and protein, they can help prevent sudden drops in blood glucose levels. In addition, they allow us to reduce our intake at traditional meal times. Smaller meals are generally easier to digest and make us more energised than big meals, which tend to make us lethargic. How often and how much are subjective, as smart snacking is not prescriptive. It's not a one-size-fits-all approach so experiment with what works for you and your kids.

3. **Sit down and eat slowly .** It's easy to lose track of what you eat and drink when you're on the run. Even with snacks, encourage your child to stop what they're doing, sit down to eat and chew properly so their body and brain registers that they have consumed something. This can help avoid overeating, and chewing food thoroughly aids the digestive process and the absorption of nutrients.

In 2009, the Organisation for Economic Co-operation and Development released a report which showed that Mexicans, Canadians and Americans are some of the fastest eaters in the world, while the French and the Turkish were the slowest. Australia was the seventh fastest – but in this race, fastest is not best![5]

4. **Be prepared.** We're pinching the motto that Robert Baden-Powell wrote for the Scouts back in 1904 because the same goes for snacks. With a little forward planning, whether that's on a Sunday, alongside preparing dinner on a weeknight or even in the morning before leaving the house, you can put together a stash of healthy snacks for your kids to have on hand when hunger hits.

5. **Choose carefully.** There are always choices, even when you're in a hurry or hungry. Make it good, better or best. Choosing to make better choices becomes a habit (and you can use our recipes as your trusty go-to options).

6. **Labels don't lie.** Read them. Look at the ingredients list and the sugar, sodium (salt) and saturated fat content. Don't get sucked in by advertising and clever marketing.

7. **Quality counts.** Wholefood snacks are a brilliant way to inject some quality nutrition into your child's day, so don't waste the opportunity to add some good stuff.

8. **Keep it real.** Choose food that looks like food, and is fresh. If it's packaged up to survive on a supermarket shelf for months, chances are it's full of preservatives and other nasties.

9. **Full-fat foods are fine.** When foods like cheese and yoghurt have the natural fat content reduced or removed, it is replaced by sugar or thickeners or both. Full-fat is fine; the only thing you need to reduce is the portion size so you still get the nutritional benefit.

10. **Look for hunger cues.** Are your children really hungry – or are they thirsty or bored? It is important to be aware of hunger cues and respond to them appropriately to avoid your kids eating snacks when not necessary.

And don't let the little ones get sucked in either – research shows that food advertising influences children's food preferences, what they ask for and what they eat. Food companies are increasingly targeting kids directly, exposing them to as many as three TV advertisements for unhealthy food in an hour![6]

HYDRATION

WHEN IT COMES TO PERFORMING WELL AT SCHOOL and during study periods, being properly hydrated is key. A human body can go three weeks without food but only about three days without water before it starts to malfunction. That's because the body is 60 per cent water. And in fact, our brain tissue is a staggering 80 per cent water. In order for the brain to function, it absolutely depends on getting enough water – the brain has no capacity to store water and so however much gets lost or used during the course of a day needs to be replaced or else cognitive functioning is impeded. What most people don't know is that the cells in your brain require *twice the energy* of other cells in the body, and guess what? Water supplies that energy.

The recommended daily fluid intake is: 5 glasses (1 litre) for children aged 5–8 years; 7 glasses (1.5 litres) for 9–12 years; 8–10 glasses (2 litres) for 13+ years.

So what can parents do to promote good hydration? Try and encourage everyone in the family to have at least one glass of water before breakfast, and then another one before they race out the door to sports practice, school or work. Always pack a full water bottle with their lunchbox, too. However, it's often hard to know how much younger kids drink, and sending them to school with a drink bottle doesn't guarantee that they will drink it or that it will get refilled during the day. Drinks spill and bottles get lost or left behind, so one strategy is to encourage kids to use the bubblers (water fountains) that are around the school grounds. Each morning at the school gate, I tell my eight-year-old son to have eight drinks of water at the bubblers during the day. (The same goes for mums and dads: just head to your office or kitchen tap eight times in the day.) But don't worry too much if you have a crazy busy day and realise you or your family haven't drunk your daily quota of water. It's not the end of the world, but if you can try and string together more days where you *have* drunk plenty, it's better. Life's not perfect, so just aim for 'positive'.

Don't forget it's important to drink in winter, too! We still need water in the cooler seasons of the year, especially when we spend time in heated rooms. It doesn't have to be cold water – a mug of boiled but slightly cooled water can be warming and easier to drink than cold water.

There's an app for that, Flip! In fact, there are several out there – they're great for reminding you to have regular drinks of water and can be used to set goals and track your intake.

Choosing drinks

Drinks provide excellent opportunities to squeeze some added nutrients into your child's day. Apart from tasting delicious, the smoothies and juices in chapter 2 (page 50) are a great way to get an extra serve (or three!) of fruit and veg into reluctant eaters. However, some drinks can be a sure-fire way to quickly ingest unwanted sugars, fats and chemicals that are not only lacking in nutrition but can be detrimental to mood and memory. Convenient and tempting though it might be for kids and teens to grab a soft drink or 'slushie' on the way home, it can come at a mental and physical cost in both the short and long term. One of the biggest concerns around these drinks is their sugar content. The World Health Organization recommends no more than 6–9 teaspoons of added sugar per day for adults and fewer than 6 teaspoons per day for children. However, one 600 ml soft drink can contain 16 teaspoons of sugar, while a 'large' (650 ml) slushie or Slurpee-style drink from a fast food or convenience store can have 21 teaspoons of sugar in it, and a 'mega' size (1.15 litre) drink of this kind can contain a whopping 38 teaspoons of sugar! Added sugars and sweeteners are also commonly found in commercially produced flavoured milks (including iced coffee), iced teas, 'vitamin' waters and sports drinks.

It's not just that – sugary drinks have also been found to have a distinctly adverse effect on the brain. Recent research in rats (which have a similar cortical architecture to humans) demonstrates that the teen brain is at an elevated risk of developing thinking problems. The investigation found that adolescent rats that imbibed sugary beverages were less able to remember a specific location leading to an escape hatch. This was compared to adult rats drinking sugary beverages, and teenage rats that had low-sugar diets. The sugar-quaffing rodents also showed increased levels of inflammation in the hippocampus, disrupting learning and memory function.

In the short term, kids who drink too many soft drinks can get what I refer to as 'soft-drunk': the sugar immediately affects their ability to think clearly and impacts on their mood. Meanwhile, the longer-term health consequences of drinks high in sugar include weight gain and associated health issues like diabetes and tooth decay.

The best advice we can give is to read the labels and avoid getting sucked in by the marketing hype. Soft drink and energy drink companies are in the business of making money, not looking after your child's wellbeing. For more info about the impact of these drinks, check out websites like rethinksugarydrink.org.au and howmuchsugar.com, David Gillespie's book *Sweet Poison* and the movie *That Sugar Film*. And if in doubt, stick to water!

TIME (AND COST) SAVING TIPS

WE ARE ALL BUSY, so finding a few time-saving tips is like finding gold! There are lots of things we can do now to help save time later, and many of these time-saving tips actually help cut costs too – a real bonus.

Sunday is my planning and preparation day. I love getting lots of things ready for the days ahead so I have less to think about when the week is underway. Setting aside time once a week is a very efficient way to tackle this task and I always find doing this on a day when I am not time-pressured is best. It doesn't have to be a Sunday; a friend of mine chooses to do all her food preparation on Monday nights because that's the night when she is almost always at home and her kids don't have any sporting or other commitments. She cooks and serves an early dinner then sets about getting ready for the week. Another friend bundles her two boys into the car on a Saturday and takes them to a farmers' market and supermarket, with the reasoning that they are the ones eating most of the food in the house and so they need to have some involvement in the shopping and know the cost and origins of their food. She makes it a really fun day and then the afternoon is spent cooking and preparing food together for the week. I really like this approach. While it may seem quicker and easier not to take the kids, if you do they'll probably be the first among their friends to start shopping for and cooking meals independently!

So do I! The formation of regular family rituals has been found to strengthen families. Family rituals help to create a sense of belonging and identity, and are positively associated with a child's socioemotional, language, academic and social skill development. When practised regularly, rituals strengthen the connectedness between partners, and parents and their children, helping to build better family bonds.

Here are some of the things you can do to give yourself a head start:

1. Look for stalls at your local fresh food market that sell boxes of fruit and veg for ridiculously cheap prices at the end of the day, especially on a Sunday. Back at home, divide the fruit and veg into portions and **freeze to use later**. Once frozen, most fruits lose their structure and texture so they are not so good to eat raw, but they are perfect for baked goodies and for adding a thick and creamy texture to smoothies. Having these fruits at the ready will help to get a smart snack whipped up in minutes. Peel bananas, chop into bitesized pieces and store portions in zip lock bags, or peel and line them up side by side, so you can easily separate them as needed for my Baked Bananas (see recipe page 106) or Bananarama Ice-Cream (see recipe page 131). Mangoes also freeze well: chop off the cheeks and, using a knife, criss-cross the flesh into even-sized squares. Use a spoon to scoop out the flesh from the skins and remove all the flesh from around the stone, then put it in zip lock bags for freezing. For pineapples, remove the spiky top and base and cut off the skin. Cut the flesh off from around the core. Discard the core then chop the flesh into bite-sized pieces and put in zip lock bags for freezing. Frozen avocados are best used for smoothies and guacamole – cut in half and carefully remove the stone, then skin

You could also try out reusable silicone storage bags for a more environmentally friendly alternative.[7]

and chop into quarters and put in zip lock bags for freezing. Portion berries into 'smoothie' amounts or large handfuls (approximately ½ cup). Watermelon is perfect for freezing due to its high water content – chop into even-sized pieces or use a melon baller to make balls, then freeze in zip lock bags.

2. Cook a big pot of **brown rice** and divide into ½–1 cup portions and freeze, ready for the Brown Rice, Coconut Oil and Hemp Seeds recipe on page 110.

3. Make several batches of **Tamari Nuts** (see recipe page 160). Once cooled, divide into portions or required batch sizes and store in the freezer. For a speedier option, just put handfuls (30–50 g) of mixed **nuts and seeds** into small zip lock bags for freezing. If not freezing, always store nuts and seeds in a consistently cool, dark place. A cupboard or pantry is fine, especially if you live in a cool–moderate climate, but I like to keep most of my nuts and seeds in the fridge. And while it's tempting to buy 'value' or big packets of nuts and seeds, make sure you have a need for them and are able to store them properly, otherwise they can get infested with pantry moths or become rancid and you'll end up throwing them out.

4. Prepare a batch of **Strawberry Chia Pots** (see recipe page 182) to see you through the early days of the week (they're best eaten within a few days of making).

5. Make **double batches** of as many balls and bars as you can. Chapter One (page 30) is full of delicious and nutritious recipes, most of which will store well in the fridge for a week or two and longer in the freezer.

6. When roasting veggies, get into the habit of always making a **double quantity**. That way you can make Roasted Veg Super Sangas (see recipe page 143) and Roasted Veg Frittatas (see recipe page 105) with minimal prep in the following days.

7. Make **big batches** of Gremolata, Red Pesto and nut butter spreads (see Chapter 8) as these all store well for long periods of time in the fridge owing to their oil content, which acts like a preservative. They make great homemade gifts in a little jar dressed up with a big ribbon – give a jar to a friend as a thank you, a foodie trade or for no reason at all. Who doesn't love receiving a handmade, practical, edible gift?

8. **Hard boil eggs** for individual snacks (see Super-Speedy Egg recipe, page 120 and Boiled Egg recipe, page 152) or to use as a filling in a Super Sanga (see Eggsellent recipe, page 141). To save time and effort, I usually cook five eggs at a time as that's how many fit into my small saucepan. Mark the shell so you (and everyone else) know it's been cooked – I use an X or draw faces on them! While it's best to store fresh or boiled eggs in their own egg carton in the main part of the fridge for a consistently cool temperature, I like to store cooked peeled eggs in an airtight container in the fridge so they don't absorb the strong flavours and smells of other food in the fridge. Boiled eggs still in their shell can last up to a week in the fridge, though I prefer to use them as close to cooking as possible. Don't bother freezing boiled eggs as the whites tend to go a bit rubbery and become tasteless.

9. **Pit and halve medjool dates** to use in smoothies (see page 50) or ball recipes (see page 30). If dicing the dates, keep and store the pips with the flesh so you know how many dates are in each zip lock bag. Store in the fridge for several weeks and the freezer for several months.

10. Buy a **loaf of bread** (especially when it's on sale and close to its 'best before' date), slice, and separate each slice of bread with pieces of greaseproof baking paper slightly bigger than the slices themselves. Return to the plastic sleeve or a zip lock bag and store in the freezer. This makes the pieces easy to separate and prevents any dangerous knife misuse! See Chapter 8 (page 136) for my favourite sandwich suggestions.

11. **Buy in bulk** and when products are on sale to take advantage of lower prices. This means you can cook in bulk which is more time-effective, as you're only preparing the ingredients and washing up once.

12. A **well-stocked pantry** with 'essentials' and some key ingredients for making smart snacks will always save you time and energy wondering if you have got something or not. A magnetic shopping list (with attached pen!) on the fridge helps to ensure that when things run out, they go on the list immediately.

13. Buy a fridge with a **big freezer** or even invest in a chest freezer to provide more space for storing pre-prepared food.

14. Containers and zip lock bags are perfect for **storing food**. I use clear containers so the contents are visible as soon as you open the fridge or freezer or pantry – opening containers to look inside is a waste of time! I also like to have my fridge and pantry neatly

stacked with a dedicated place for each ingredient and product, so I know at a glance what's there and what's missing. This means no time is wasted moving tins or jars around looking for something.

15. **Write notes** on the fridge or containers letting everyone in the family know what's available to eat and when! This saves time used on decision-making and helps manage what's in the fridge so it's eaten at the intended time.

DEALING WITH THE STRESS OF STUDY

YEARS AGO, JUST AROUND THE TIME THEY INVENTED ELECTRICITY (but way before Facebook, Snapchat and Instagram), I did my final year of school. My parents were working in New Zealand at the time and the boffins at the New Zealand Department of Education had decided to abolish Year 12 exams. Instead, your chances of going to university were assessed on the basis of how well you did on essays and tests throughout the year. The result was a very cruisy year, with little emotional trauma.

Fast forward to January 2003, when the New South Wales Commissioner for Children and Young People called for an urgent investigation into how best to support young people during the final years of school. This came after the state government Child Death Review Team commissioned an expert report analysing 111 adolescent suicides in New South Wales. The report found that pressure to perform in Year 12 contributed to one in eleven adolescent suicides in the state.[8]

Three years later, a Victorian study found that nearly one in five Year 12 students had thought about killing or hurting themselves because of pressure.[9] Psychologist Karen McGraw carried out a Swinburne University study and found that stress and its impact on the students were alarming. Of the 940 final year students surveyed, 19 per cent had thoughts of suicide or self-harm, about a third were severely depressed, and 41 per cent suffered from anxiety.

In December 2017, Mission Australia surveyed over 24 000 15–19-year-olds and found that almost 45 per cent said they were very concerned or extremely concerned about study and school – the highest level since the survey started in 2002. Every year, it seems more and more emphasis is placed on achieving good results in the end-of-school exams, and this can lead to students feeling extraordinary pressure and having unrealistic expectations. So, times have certainly changed, and it appears that sadly many young people believe that they *are* their ATAR (Australian Tertiary Admission Rank – the score that determines a student's entry into university) and that their life will not be worth living unless they get 99.95.

My philosophy is that studying at school is a little like playing a game of Monopoly and if you know the tricks (buy railroads early) you can swing the odds of succeeding in your favour. So, what are the tricks that sit alongside the idea of smart snacking? These are my top tips for all secondary school students during this testing time:

Try to get enough sleep

For all students, the single most important study tool is a good night's sleep. Research demonstrates that staying up late in an attempt to memorise extra facts has the opposite effect, giving the brain no 'downtime' to embed its knowledge. In a new study, researchers tracked students taking major exams and correlated their marks with the number of hours they slept the night before.[10] Not too surprisingly, they found that sleep deprivation corresponded to lower exam scores. Most importantly, sleep helps your brain to assimilate new knowledge into your long-term memory so that you can recall it when it comes to test day. Anyone who has tried to concentrate with half a night's sleep can also testify to improved focus with better sleep.

Exercise before an exam

Research has shown that exercising can aid your memory and brain power. It's been scientifically proven that taking a 20-minute walk before an exam can boost your cognitive performance by up to 10 per cent: a study by Charles Hillman of the University of Illinois found that moderate exercise (30 minutes for adults and 20 minutes for children) can result in a 5–10 per cent improvement in cognition, the activity that takes place in the brain's frontal lobe.[11]

Take breaks every 20 minutes

On average, our brains are not designed to remain focused on a single task for a significantly long time – most people usually begin to lose focus and concentration after 20 minutes. Their quality of reception starts to drop and their ability to adequately grasp information from their point of attention deteriorates. At this point, their brain requires some time off, a distraction. Bear this in mind when planning your study and try to take regular breaks – it's a more efficient way to work.

Use a mindfulness app

Meditation is one of the most effective ways to take a break and view your stress from a different angle. Practising mindfulness meditation is a great way to maintain focus while improving both mental and physical wellbeing to reduce pre-exam stress.

Go cold turkey on tech

It can be hard to disconnect from your online world while studying but keeping the end goal and timeframe in mind will ease the process. Rather than relying on your willpower, try internet-blocking applications like Cold Turkey that block distractions such as apps or websites for certain periods of time within your schedule. They can be fantastic for improving focus and productivity.

Say it out loud

A paper by Colin MacLeod and colleagues in the *Journal of Experimental Psychology: Learning, Memory, and Cognition* in 2010 looked at people's memory for items like a list of words.[12] In their experiments, they found that if people studied the list by reading half of the words silently and saying the other half out loud, the words spoken aloud were remembered much better than those that were read silently. This is known as the 'production effect' and it can be a great technique for improving your memory of certain information during study.

Taking notes? Don't use a laptop

Did you know that taking notes with pen and paper (the old-fashioned way) actually enhances memory and your capacity to understand whatever it is that you are studying? Researchers from Princeton and UCLA studied students in classrooms where some took notes with laptops and others with pen and paper. They discovered that taking notes using a tablet or computer could be damaging to academic performance as students who did so were more likely to transcribe 'mindlessly', resulting in shallower learning. Students using pen and paper showed they had learned and retained more understanding in the long run.[13]

Have breakfast

Food is energy and knowing what to eat and drink before studying or taking exams can make all the difference to your performance. Missing breakfast can impair your cognitive function and capacity to study, while evidence suggests that breakfast consumption – when compared to skipping breakfast – enhances cognitive function in all students. Particularly good breakfast foods include full-fat plain yoghurt, blueberries, eggs and wholefood cereals such as porridge and natural muesli. If you find it hard to manage a substantial meal in the morning, at the very least try one of Flip's delicious smoothies (see page 50).

Eat dark chocolate

Consuming dark chocolate (with over 70 per cent cocoa content) can help buffer the effects of the stress hormone cortisol.[14] Make sure you only consume it in moderate amounts, though!

Remember: not all stress is bad

When I was at school, stress was actually an architectural term referring to bridges and no one used the term much in the way it's used today. A small amount of stress can actually be good for you and can improve the efficiency of your performance. If you have very little stress it can lead to boredom and depression, while an excess can cause anxiety and poor health. According to the Yerkes–Dodson law, some amount of stress is needed to push you to the level for optimal alertness and behavioural and cognitive performance.[15] In other words, the right amount of acute stress tunes up the brain and improves performance and health – so try not to think of it as a completely bad thing and instead harness it to help you.

RECIPE LIST

CACAO BALLS

OAT BALLS

CASHEW BALLS

CHAI-SPICED SUNFLOWER SEED BALLS

BANANA BALLS

ZESTY COCONUT BALLS

APRICOT BALLS

GLUTEN-FREE APRICOT BALLS

PRUNE AND WALNUT BALLS

HEMP SEED BALLS

HUMMUS BALLS

MATCHA BALLS

CHOCOLATE COCONUT BALLS

TAHINI BALLS

1

ON THE BALL

ENERGY BALLS ARE THE ULTIMATE SNACKS because they are dead easy to make, they are packed full of nutritional goodies, and you can make a big batch and be snack-ready for the week.

Sunday afternoons are a great time to make a big batch of balls because they can then be divided into several zip lock bags and allocated to the different days of the week. Written notes on the bags like 'Monday afternoon tea', 'Before footy' or 'After piano' let everyone know when the balls can be eaten and this (mostly!) prevents them from disappearing prematurely. The other benefit of dividing up the balls into separate bags is that it's harder to scoff too many in one sitting – which is a risk because they are so delicious and moreish!

The action of rolling the mixture into balls can also be really relaxing. Think of these balls as culinary stress busters – the contraction and relaxation of your hands can help to calm mind and body. So, when the kids have had a bad day at school, are feeling stressed from exams or need some downtime after a day of sport, encourage them to make a batch of energy balls. Not only do they get to eat something delicious and nutritious when their creations are complete, but they will hopefully have a more positive mindset by the time they take their first bite.

Dates make great natural sweeteners proven to decrease cholesterol, prevent and relieve constipation, reduce triglyceride levels and boost bone health.

Medjool dates are a star ingredient in many of my ball recipes. Not only are they naturally sweet but they are also ideal for binding all the other nutritionally dense ingredients together. They have a soft texture and a rich, caramel flavour – however, any other date varieties can be used in place of medjool. (Dates are also a great source of fibre to fill you up and keep you regular!) If your dates are a bit dry, simply soak them in hot or boiling water for about 10 minutes or until soft, then drain before using them.

Coconut also appears regularly in my ball recipes – in desiccated, shredded and oil forms – because it's naturally sweet and has a wonderful flavour.

A couple of tips: if you make a batch of balls that seems too sticky, just add more nuts, chia seeds or coconut (a little at a time); and if the mixture is too crumbly, add more sticky stuff like dates.

While it's not a deal breaker, all of these balls are best served after being chilled for approximately 30 minutes so that they're firm and the flavours have had a chance to intensify.

There are fourteen fantastic ball recipes in this chapter. Why not try my never-fail favourite Cacao Balls (see page 34)? My Cashew Balls (see page 37) only require two ingredients to create a creamy treat, or give the Chocolate Coconut Balls (see page 48) a go – they're nut-free and therefore perfect for school lunches.

So, what are you waiting for? A delicious and nutritious snack is just minutes away!

CACAO BALLS

dairy-free / egg-free / gluten-free / grain-free / wheat-free / freezable

My eight-year-old son adores these chocolatey balls and I have to admit they're my favourite snack, too! We make a batch together most weeks. I'd like to say the batch makes 20 small balls but I can't be completely sure because we always end up eating some of the mixture before the balls make it into the container! The chilli powder is a great addition for those that love something spicy, but obviously don't add this if your kids don't like anything too hot! If you do decide to use chilli, I recommend adding the sea salt too as this is a fab flavour combo which also makes an excellent after dinner treat for adults served with coffee!

Makes 20 (I think!)

2 cups (200 g) walnuts
¼ cup (20 g) shredded coconut
2 tablespoons cacao powder (for a very rich chocolate taste, use ¼ cup)
1 tablespoon chia seeds

1 teaspoon ground cinnamon
¼–½ teaspoon mild chilli powder (optional)
pinch of sea salt (optional)
2½ cups (450 g) medjool dates, pitted (about 23)

1. Put the walnuts, coconut, caco, chia seeds, cinnamon, chilli powder and salt (if using) into a food processor and process until finely chopped. With the motor running, start adding the dates a few at a time until all have been incorporated and the mixture has a crumbly consistency. If you like a smoother consistency, process for longer.

2. Transfer the mixture to a bowl for safety and ease of working.
3. Using your fingers or a measuring spoon, grab approximately 2 tablespoons of mixture, and roll into a ball. Repeat with the remaining mixture to make 20 balls.
4. Cover and chill in the fridge for 30 minutes , if you can resist, before eating.

TIP: Cacao Balls can be kept in an airtight container in the fridge for up to 1 week or the freezer for 1 month.

You could use this chilling time to replicate the famous marshmallow experiment, a series of studies on delayed gratification in the late 1960s and early 1970s led by psychologist Walter Mischel. Mischel offered kids a choice between one marshmallow immediately or two marshmallows if they waited for a short period, approximately 15 minutes, during which the boffin in a white coat left the room and then returned. In follow-up studies, the researchers found that children who demonstrated an ability to be patient had better life outcomes, as measured by educational attainment, body mass index, and marital satisfaction!

OAT BALLS

egg-free / wheat-free

Rolled oats are a complex carbohydrate that provide a slow release of energy. If you or the kids don't have time for a big sit-down brekkie, grab a couple of these on the way out the door. This recipe is easy to remember because it's around 100 g each of the four main ingredients.

Makes 18–20

The sole source of energy for the growing brain is glucose, which comes from carbohydrates – that's why breakkie is so important. These oat balls are pure brain energy food.

Ricotta cheese has a similar consistency to cottage cheese but it's lighter and only ½ cup contains 25 per cent of our daily calcium needs. It's also low in sodium but high in vitamins A and B, phosphorus and zinc – brain bliss!

1 cup (90) g rolled (traditional) oats
1 cup (100 g) walnuts
1 teaspoon ground cinnamon
100 g medjool dates, pitted (about 9)

⅔ cup (100 g) ricotta cheese
⅓ cup (25 g) desiccated coconut (you can use shredded but desiccated coats the balls better)

Walnuts are the top nut for brain health: they have a significantly high concentration of DHA, a type of omega-3 fatty acid which has been shown to protect brain health in babies and improve cognitive performance in kids. They also boast almost twice as many antioxidants as other commonly consumed nuts such as almonds, peanuts and pistachios.

1. Put the oats, walnuts and cinnamon into a food processor and process until finely chopped. With the motor running, start adding the dates a few at a time until all have been incorporated. Add the ricotta and process again until the mixture comes together and forms a ball.

2. Transfer mixture to a bowl for safety and ease of working. Using your fingers or a measuring spoon, grab approximately 2 tablespoons of mixture, and roll into a ball. Repeat with remaining mixture to make 18–20 balls.

3. Put coconut in a shallow bowl. Roll each ball in coconut to lightly coat. Cover and chill in the fridge for 30 minutes before eating.

TIP: Oat Balls and Cashew Balls (opposite) keep in an airtight container in the fridge for up to 1 week.

CASHEW BALLS

dairy-free / egg-free / gluten-free /
grain-free / wheat-free / freezable

All you need for this creamy treat are two ingredients – dates and cashews ! I love these balls as they are but to change it up I sometimes add a little freshly grated ginger and turmeric for their wonderful calming effects and flavour. With the addition of these spices, the balls taste like gingerbread dough! If you don't have the spices in fresh form, try using ½ teaspoon ground ginger and ¼ teaspoon ground turmeric . Another way to mix things up is to roll the balls in desiccated coconut, sesame seeds or poppy seeds . Adding small but high-impact foods to your snacks is a simple, tasty way to boost every bite.

Makes 18

1 cup (130 g) raw, unsalted cashews

1 cup (180 g) medjool dates, pitted (about 9)

1. Put cashews into a food processor and process until finely chopped. With the motor running, start adding the dates a few at a time until all have been incorporated and the mixture comes together to form a ball.
2. Transfer mixture to a bowl for safety and ease of working. Using your fingers or a measuring spoon, roll approximately 2 tablespoons of mixture into a ball. Repeat with remaining mixture to make 18 balls.
3. Cover and chill in the fridge for 30 minutes before eating.

I am a big fan of cashews – not just because they are a tiny collection of iron, magnesium, vitamin B6, protein and important amino acids, and even omega-3 fats, but also because their tryptophan content may have a limited benefit in the treatment of depression.

Flip, did you know that ginger has been found to lead to improvements in working memory?

Curcumin is a bioactive ingredient in turmeric, capable of journeying across the blood–brain barrier – which is one reason why it holds promise as a neuroprotective agent in a wide range of neurological disorders.

While the tiny poppy seed may look unassuming, it actually contains calcium and magnesium which help regulate brain activity and aid in the development of brain cells – so don't judge a book by its cover!

CHAI-SPICED SUNFLOWER SEED BALLS

dairy-free / egg-free / gluten-free / grain-free / nut-free / wheat-free / freezable

I love the flavour and aroma of chai so I have added it to these balls. I like sunflower seeds for this recipe but you could also use any nuts you like (cashews work well).

Makes 20–25

2 cups (300 g) sunflower
    seeds
pinch of sea salt
1 teaspoon ground
    cinnamon
½ teaspoon ground ginger

¼ teaspoon nutmeg
¼ teaspoon ground cloves
1 cup (180 g) medjool dates,
    pitted (about 9)
2–3 tablespoons coconut
    oil, melted

1. Put seeds, salt and spices into a food processor and process until finely chopped. With the motor running, start adding the dates a few at a time until all have been incorporated. Add 2 tablespoons coconut oil and process again until the mixture comes together and forms a ball (adding a little extra oil if necessary).
2. Transfer the mixture to a bowl for safety and ease of working. Using your fingers or a measuring spoon, roll 2 tablespoons of mixture into a ball. Repeat with the remaining mixture to make 20–25 balls.
3. Cover and chill in the fridge for 30 minutes to allow the flavours to infuse before eating.

TIP: You can swap the ground spices with 2 teaspoons chai spice blend.

Did you know that chai has been treasured for centuries in India because of its ability to aid digestion? More brain blessedness!

Sunflower seeds contain an amino acid that can help boost serotonin levels and alleviate stress.

Nutmeg contains the mysterious-sounding myristicin and macelignan, compounds which may reduce the degradation of neural pathways and may help keep the brain functioning at a normal, healthy level.

BANANA BALLS

dairy-free / egg-free / nut-free / wheat-free / freezable

A good mood is guaranteed with these delish and super easy balls. Bananas are packed full of potassium, which is a natural mood elevator. The riper the banana you use to make these, the sweeter the taste and the softer the texture of the balls.

Makes 12–15

1 large banana, peeled
1 cup (90 g) quick oats
1 cup (70 g) shredded
 coconut
1 teaspoon ground
 cinnamon

1 teaspoon vanilla extract
¼ cup (25 g) cacao powder
 (or you can use sesame
 seeds)

Oh, and so much more! The average banana has less than half a gram of fat, no cholesterol, about 2.5 grams of fibre and 0.4 milligrams of vitamin B6. Preliminary laboratory studies indicate that bananas may invigorate memory performance – what's not to love?[16]

1. Mash the banana with a fork in a medium-sized bowl. Add oats, shredded coconut, cinnamon and vanilla and stir until well combined. This mixture is very thick so I tend to roll up my sleeves and use my hands. It's great to feel it squelching through your fingers! Kids love doing this, too.

2. Using your fingers or a measuring spoon, roll approximately 2 tablespoons of mixture into a ball. Repeat with remaining mixture to make 12–15 balls.

3. Put cacao (or sesame seeds) in a shallow bowl. Roll each ball in cacao to lightly coat. Cover and chill in the fridge for 30 minutes before eating.

TIP: Banana Balls and Chai-Spiced Sunflower Seed Balls (opposite) can be kept in an airtight container in the fridge for up to 1 week or in the freezer for 1 month.

ZESTY COCONUT BALLS

dairy-free / egg-free / gluten-free /
grain-free / wheat-free / freezable

I love lemons and add them to everything – which sends
my husband nuts. I actually use the zest of two lemons
for this recipe but just use one if you'd like the flavour a
little less intense. The chia seeds look like ants so my son
Harvey sometimes calls these 'squashed ant balls'.

Makes about 22

2 cups (140 g) shredded
   coconut
1 cup (160 g) almonds
finely grated zest of 1 lemon
¼ cup (60 ml) lemon juice
¼ cup (60 g) coconut oil,
   melted

1 tablespoon honey
1 tablespoon chia seeds
¼ cup (30 g) sesame seeds
   (or poppy seeds or chia
   seeds), or 2 tablespoons
   desiccated coconut for
   coating (optional)

1. Put all ingredients (except seeds or coconut for coating)
   into a food processor and process for a minute or two or
   until the mixture is well combined.
2. Transfer mixture to a bowl for safety and ease of
   working. Using your fingers or a measuring spoon,
   roll approximately 2 tablespoons of mixture into a ball.
   Repeat with remaining mixture to make 22 balls.
3. If coating the balls, place seeds (or coconut) in a high-
   sided bowl. Place balls in the bowl and gently move the
   bowl in a circular direction so they become evenly coated
   in sesame seeds.
4. Cover and chill in the fridge for about 30 minutes
   before eating.

APRICOT BALLS

dairy-free / egg-free / nut-free /
wheat-free / freezable

Apricot balls are traditionally made with condensed
milk, but I use coconut oil to make this a much healthier
version. You can roll them very lightly in ground turmeric
to amp up their nutritional value – and the intensity
of their orange colour.

Makes 18–20

2 cups (300 g) dried apricot
   halves (I like yummy
   Australian apricots best)
1 cup (70 g) shredded
   coconut

½ cup (45 g) rolled
   (traditional) oats
⅓ cup (75 g) coconut oil,
   melted

Aussie, Aussie, Aussie! Love
your patriotism, Flip. Apricots
are chockers with vitamin A,
which is important for normal
vision, proper immune system
function and reproduction,
as well as maintaining
healthy skin, teeth, and
skeletal and soft tissue.

1. Put all ingredients into a food processor and process
   for a minute or two or until the mixture is well combined
   and comes together to form a ball.
2. Transfer mixture to a bowl for safety and ease of
   working. Using your fingers or a measuring spoon,
   roll approximately 2 tablespoons of mixture into a ball.
   Give the ball a good squeeze to ensure it binds. Repeat
   with remaining mixture to make 18–20 balls.
3. Cover and chill in the fridge for about 30 minutes
   before eating.

**TIP: Apricot Balls and Zesty Coconut Balls (opposite)
can be kept in an airtight container in the fridge for
up to 1 week or in the freezer for 1 month.**

GLUTEN-FREE APRICOT BALLS

dairy-free / egg-free / gluten-free /
grain-free / wheat-free / freezable

**And now for the gluten-free version of my apricot balls –
otherwise my godsons, Jez and Ed, and husband,
Joffa, will kill me!**

Makes 18–20

Almonds have been prized since ancient times as one of humankind's most treasured nuts. Ayurvedic practitioners maintain that nuts are capable of increasing brain capacity, intellectual ability and longevity – and there may be some truth to their assertions! Almonds are a source of vitamin E, copper, magnesium and protein.

1 cup (150 g) dried apricot
  halves
1 cup (70 g) shredded
  coconut

1 cup (160 g) almonds
⅓ cup (75 g) coconut oil,
  melted
dash of vanilla extract

1. Put all ingredients into a food processor and process for a minute or two or until the mixture is well combined and comes together to form a ball.
2. Transfer mixture to a bowl for safety and ease of working. Using your fingers or a measuring spoon, roll approximately 2 tablespoons of mixture into a ball. Repeat with remaining mixture to make 18–20 balls.
3. Cover and chill in the fridge for about 30 minutes before eating.

TIP: Gluten-Free Apricot Balls can be kept in an airtight container in the fridge for up to 1 week or freezer for 1 month.

PRUNE AND WALNUT BALLS (A.K.A. PRUNUT BALLS)

dairy-free / egg-free / gluten-free /
grain-free / wheat-free / freezable

I love prunes but they sometimes get a bum rap (if you'll excuse the pun). Yes, most of us know they are high in fibre and help keep you regular, but they are also delicious and contain as many antioxidants as blueberries. They may also be good for your heart and skin . Maybe we should simply call them dried plums – which is what they are!

Makes about 15

1 cup (170 g) pitted prunes
1 cup (100 g) walnuts
½ cup (75 g) dried apricot
   halves

¼ cup (20 g) shredded
   coconut
1 teaspoon ground
   cinnamon

1. Put all ingredients into a food processor and process for a minute or two or until the mixture is well combined and comes together to form a ball.
2. Transfer mixture to a bowl for safety and ease of working. Using your fingers or a measuring spoon, roll approximately 2 tablespoons of mixture into a ball. Repeat with remaining mixture to make about 15 balls.
3. Cover and chill in the fridge for about 30 minutes before eating.

TIP: Prunut Balls can be kept in an airtight container in the fridge for up to 1 week or freezer for 1 month.

Yep, and they contain stratospheric levels of phenols, which act as antioxidants to promote healthy ageing by minimising DNA damage caused by free radicals.

Flip, the California Prune Board – yes, there is one – must have heard you! They compelled the US Food and Drug Administration to alter the name of prunes to the more appealing 'dried plums' – and it worked! Following the name change, sales went through the roof!

To ancient Egyptians, cinnamon was more valuable than gold as they believed it to have immense medical potential. Today, it remains a readily available source of powerful antioxidant properties, and in animal studies has been shown to lead to brain function improvements for Alzheimer's and Parkinson's disease. One animal study found that merely smelling cinnamon can improve performance in several types of cognitive tasks.[17]

HEMP SEED BALLS

dairy-free / egg-free / gluten-free / grain-free /
nut-free / wheat-free / freezable

Boffins who study diets say that seeds are important to include in the diet, and the message is getting through to the point that it is now almost normal to sprinkle a teaspoon of flaxseed (an excellent source of omega-3) or sunflower seeds (high in immune-supportive zinc) into soups, salads, yoghurt and cereals.

Move over, chia seeds, hemp is the new kid on the block. Now legalised as a food, hemp contains exceptionally high levels of omega-3 and -6. Meanwhile, maca is believed to improve mood, reduce stress and anxiety, and increase stamina and energy levels. And we could all do with that! Both maca and hemp can be found in most health food stores and are becoming more available in supermarkets.

Makes about 15

1 cup (135 g) hemp seeds
1 cup (180 g) medjool dates, pitted (about 9)
3 teaspoons maca powder (optional)

1 teaspoon ground cinnamon
pinch of sea salt

1. Put all ingredients into a food processor and process for a minute or two or until the mixture is well combined and comes together to form a ball.
2. Transfer mixture to a bowl for safety and ease of working. Using your fingers or a measuring spoon, roll approximately 2 tablespoons of mixture into a ball. Repeat with remaining mixture to make about 15 balls.
3. Cover and chill in the fridge for about 30 minutes before eating.

TIP: Hemp Seed Balls and Hummus Balls (opposite) can be kept in an airtight container in the fridge for up to 1 week or in the freezer for 1 month.

HUMMUS BALLS

dairy-free / egg-free / gluten-free / nut-free / wheat-free / freezable

I love hummus dip and these balls are (almost) better! They are soft like a truffle but not very sweet as I only use a couple of dates. If you want the balls to be firmer, add ¼ cup of shredded coconut, protein powder, almond meal or lucuma – a powder from South America full of antioxidants with a naturally sweet taste. Have fun and play with the flavours.

Makes 15–18

400 g can chickpeas, rinsed, drained
¼ cup (60 g) tahini (at room temperature)
2–3 medjool dates, pitted

½ teaspoon ground cinnamon
1 tablespoon sesame seeds or cacao powder, for coating (optional)

1. Process chickpeas, tahini, dates and cinnamon in a food processor for a minute or two or until the mixture is well combined and comes together to form a ball.
2. Transfer mixture to a bowl for safety and ease of working. Using your fingers or a measuring spoon, roll approximately 2 tablespoons of mixture into a ball. Repeat with remaining mixture to make 15–18 balls.
3. If coating balls, place sesame seeds or cacao powder in a high-sided bowl. Place balls in the bowl and gently move bowl in a circular direction so they become evenly coated.
4. Cover and chill in the fridge for 30 minutes before eating.

I do love a good dip! A Mediterranean staple, hummus is rich in B vitamins and omega-3, nutrients that are essential to brain health.

Chickpeas are packed full of vitamins, minerals and fibre plus tryptophan – one of the building blocks of serotonin, and melatonin, the sleep hormone – which help make you feel fabulous and help you sleep. Two essential things for students.

MATCHA BALLS

dairy-free / egg-free / gluten-free /
grain-free / wheat-free / freezable

Though a lot of people think matcha came from Japan, Japanese zen monks actually brought tea plants home from China. Later on, matcha became the chosen thirst-quencher of samurais and the Japanese royalty and upper class, and even today it remains the only official tea used in the traditional Japanese tea ceremony.

One cup of matcha can have the antioxidant equivalent of up to 10 cups of green tea!

Matcha green tea originated in China more than 1000 years ago and is believed to be the most potent green tea in the world. Matcha is a fine powder made from special green tea leaves which you can add to smoothies, porridge or balls. It is rich in fibre and antioxidants, and full of chlorophyll. The combination of L-theanine and caffeine appears to improve concentration and memory – while reducing stimulation caused by the caffeine. I love the vibrant green colour of these matcha balls, especially if you use pistachios and roll them in extra matcha powder. If you are new to matcha, start with just 1 tablespoon in the ball mixture. Rolling the balls in extra matcha is not necessary if you don't have the time or prefer a more subtle taste.

Makes 18–20

1 cup (150–160 g) raw unsalted nuts (I like a combo of almonds, cashews and pistachios)
½ cup (35 g) shredded coconut
2 tablespoons matcha powder

2 cups (320 g) medjool dates, pitted (about 18)
1 tablespoon matcha powder, for coating (optional)
2 tablespoons finely chopped pistachos, for coating (optional)

1. Put nuts, coconut and matcha powder into a food processor and process until finely chopped. With the motor running, start adding the dates a few at a time until all have been incorporated and the mixture comes together to form a ball.

2. Transfer the mixture to a bowl for safety and ease of working. Using your fingers or a measuring spoon, roll approximately 2 tablespoons of mixture into a ball. Repeat with remaining mixture to make 18–20 balls.

3. If coating the balls, put the extra matcha in a high-sided bowl. Place balls in a bowl and gently move it in a circular direction so they become evenly and lightly coated. Or, as these balls have a dense texture and hold together well, you can put the matcha powder and balls into a medium-sized zip lock bag then gently move the balls around in the bag to lightly coat them in powder.

4. Alternative delicious coatings are finely chopped pistachios or sesame seeds.

5. Cover and chill in the fridge for about 30 minutes before eating.

TIP: These balls can be kept in an airtight container in the fridge for up to 1 week or in the freezer for 1 month.

Pistachios make great snacks as they have zero cholesterol content – though they're very energy-dense!

CHOCOLATE COCONUT BALLS

dairy-free / egg-free / nut-free /
wheat-free / freezable

Like an episode of
Game of Thrones?

**These are very rich and intense so you will only
need one at a time. They are also nut-free,
making them a good option for lunchboxes.**

Makes 18–20

Cacao has an antioxidant
score of 95 500: 14 times
more antioxidant flavonoids
than red wine, 21 times more
than green tea and 7 times
more than dark chocolate.

¼ cup (25 g) cacao powder
½ cup (40 g) shredded
  coconut
½ cup (45 g) rolled
  (traditional) oats
1 teaspoon ground
  cinnamon

2 cups (280 g) pitted fresh
  dates (about 18)
2 tablespoons desiccated
  coconut, for coating
  (optional)
1 tablespoon cacao powder,
  for coating (optional)

1. Put cacao, coconut, oats and cinnamon into a food
   processor. With the motor running, start adding the
   dates a few at a time until all have been incorporated
   and mixture starts to bind together.
2. Transfer mixture to a bowl for safety and ease of
   working. Using your fingers or a measuring spoon,
   roll approximately 2 tablespoons of mixture into a ball.
   Repeat with the remaining mixture to make 18–20 balls.
3. If coating balls, put desiccated coconut or cacao powder
   (or both!) in a high-sided bowl. Place balls in bowl and
   gently move the bowl in a circular direction so balls
   become evenly and lightly coated.
4. Cover and chill in fridge for about 30 minutes
   before eating.

TAHINI BALLS

dairy-free / egg-free / gluten-free /
grain-free / nut-free / wheat-free / freezable

These are so delicious but make them small (like the size
of a Smartie) as they are *really* rich. You can also thin out
the mixture with a little coconut oil and spread it on toast
for something sweet, or add it to porridge or a smoothie.

Makes 15–20

½ cup (120 g) tahini
  (at room temperature)
¼ cup (25 g) cacao powder

2 tablespoons coconut
  syrup
2 tablespoons desiccated
  coconut, for coating

Tahini is made from sesame
seeds, a good source of
omega-3 fatty acids.

1. Put tahini, cacao powder and coconut syrup into a food
   processor and process for a minute or two or until mixture
   is well combined and comes together to form a ball.
2. Transfer mixture to a bowl for safety and ease of
   working. Using your fingers or a measuring spoon,
   roll approximately 1 teaspoon of mixture into a ball.
   Repeat with the remaning mixture to make 15–20 balls.
3. Put desiccated coconut in a shallow bowl. Roll each ball
   in coconut to lightly coat. Cover and chill in the fridge
   for about 30 minutes before eating.

**TIP: Tahini Balls and Chocolate Coconut Balls (opposite)
can be kept in an airtight container in the fridge for up
to 1 week or freezer for 1 month.**

RECIPE LIST

ABC

AÇAÍ

SMOOSLI

I PINE FOR YOU

RASPBERRY CHIA

CHOCONANA

ZUCCHINI AND KEFIR

MANGO LASSI

IT'S EASY BEING GREEN

HIT THE TROPICS

TUMMY TONIC

BEET THE BLOAT

GET RED(DY) AND GO

KOMBUCHA 'JUICE'

SMOOTHIES & JUICES

2

SMOOTHIES ARE A BRILLIANT CHOICE for a wholesome snack and they also make a fantastic option for breakfast, lunch or a late dinner. I love the 'eat the rainbow' philosophy because it means your kids are getting a wide variety of fruit and veg – and smoothies are the perfect way to do this.

Blending fruit and veggies into a smoothie means that the fibre is broken down but not destroyed (as it is when food is juiced) so it still offers fantastic nutritional benefits. The blender performs the role of the chewing so when the liquid enters the body it can be digested quickly and easily. This is good for the times when the kids (or you!) are feeling stressed, really tired or in a rush, as these conditions negatively impact the body's ability to digest food properly. If we try to eat a lot of food at these times to bolster energy or for comfort, we can end up with a tummy ache – so this is when it's wise to grab the blender.

The other great thing about smoothies is that they are 'un- stuff-up-able'. Use the ten wholefood smoothies and four juice recipes in this chapter as a starting point but feel free to tweak them or create your own blends. Imagination and personal taste are the only limitations here! A good ratio to work with is one part liquid, one part veggies and two parts fruit. You can always use water where liquid is needed but I love to use coconut water or kombucha when it's in the fridge to give an added nutritional boost.

Stock the freezer with frozen fruit like chopped banana, mango and pineapple, blueberries and raspberries –

Did you know that the research says that 26.6 per cent of boys and 38.6 per cent of girls skip breakfast some or all of the time? Yet the brain needs fuel – all students MUST have brekkie. So for those who are reluctant, smoothies can be a great compromise.

Just remember to screw the top of the blender on properly!

Known from now on as the 'Flip Fruit Formula'!

I even freeze avocado. Frozen fruit gives smoothies a lovely thick texture and creamy taste and this way you'll have a ready stash to make an instant smoothie. Freezing very ripe fruit is also a good way to store it rather than throwing it away – but please don't use fruit that has turned and gone bad! The freezer is fantastic but it doesn't make fruit magically come back to life and you'll be filling yourself up with nutritionally compromised food.

So true, Flip – I have one every morning with frozen blueberries and banana. I love the texture.

To bulk up a smoothie, add 2 teaspoons of chia seeds, 1 tablespoon of psyllium husks or half an avocado or frozen banana. The fibre and fat will increase your level of satiety.

Psyllium is a form of fibre made from the husks of the *Plantago ovata* plant's seeds. It can act as a laxative when consumed in high volumes, so only use a tablespoon!

You don't need a really expensive blender to make a good smoothie. I bought a 220V blender for $50 three years ago because it was the smallest one I could find (I only have a little kitchen) and it just keeps going and going.

And one last tip: it's always best to drink smoothies and juices as close to the preparation time as possible. If you're leaving the house early in the morning, you can make your kids' smoothies the night before to save time. Just try not to let them sit in the fridge for any longer than 12 hours, and I wouldn't freeze them. If you do need to store a freshly made drink for later, put it in the fridge in a glass container with an airtight lid until drinking time – ensure you fill the container to the very top to prevent air from being trapped in it, as air will destroy the nutrients in the drink. You can also add a little lemon juice to prevent it from going brown. But if it smells or looks at all bad, then don't drink it!

ABC

dairy-free / egg-free / gluten-free / grain-free / nut-free / wheat-free

A.K.A. the *Sesame Street* smoothie!

Avocado, blueberries, coconut . . . plus lots more. This is the essential smoothie. You can use fresh blueberries and banana but I much prefer to use them frozen because it gives the smoothie a fantastic thick and creamy texture.

Makes 1

½ avocado
½ cup (75 g) fresh or frozen blueberries
½–1 frozen banana, chopped
1 tablespoon coconut oil, melted

1 teaspoon ground cinnamon
1 tablespoon spirulina powder or hemp seeds (optional)
1 cup (250 ml) water or coconut water

Spirulina is such an interesting substance. Said to be one of the oldest life forms on earth, it has been used medicinally since as far back as the ninth century in Chad, Africa.

1. Put all ingredients into a blender and blend until smooth. Go!

AÇAÍ

dairy-free / egg-free / gluten-free /
grain-free / nut-free / wheat-free

We lived in Brazil for two years and my son, Harvey, drank this bright purple mixture every day before we even knew how to pronounce it correctly, and before it became popular here in Australia. In Brazil, the açaí mixture is so thick you are given a spoon – not a straw – to tackle it! There, it is served in a glass (*copo*) or bowl (*tigela*) and it is also loaded with sugar and guaraná, so my recipe is a healthier version. Like the ABC smoothie on the opposite page, using frozen blueberries and banana gives the smoothie a delicious thick and creamy texture.

Makes 1

1 tablespoon açaí powder (see Tip)
½ teaspoon ground cinnamon
1 frozen banana, chopped
½ cup (75 g) fresh or frozen blueberries
¼ cup (60 ml) coconut water
2–3 ice cubes
1 pitted medjool date (optional)

1. Put all ingredients into a blender and blend until smooth. If you prefer a thinner consistency, add a little more coconut water.

TIP: You can buy açaí powder or frozen açaí from health food stores and some supermarkets in the 'health food' or freezer sections. One 100 g portion of frozen açaí is equivalent to 1 tablespoon of powder and will give your smoothie a thick consistency.

A recent study conducted at the University of Adelaide found that certain polyphenols from açaí berries may inhibit the formation of plaque from beta-amyloid proteins.[18] One of the characteristics of Alzheimer's disease is the build-up of amyloid plaques between brain cells. Beta amyloid comes from a larger protein found in the fatty membrane surrounding nerve cells and is chemically 'sticky', making it gradually build up into plaques. In a healthy brain, these protein fragments are broken down and eliminated.

SMOOSLI

dairy-free (option) / egg-free / wheat-free

No time for breakfast? Well, this is the answer – muesli + smoothie = smoosli! Frozen banana makes this smoothie thick and creamy, but fresh banana is fine to use. I find that we tend to drink cold smoothies more slowly, which is better for digestion and allows the brain the time to register that we've eaten something. Maca is a cruciferous vegetable originating in Peru. The edible part of the plant is the root, which is then dried and turned into a powder that can be added to smoothies or porridge. It has a nutty, earthy flavour which isn't everyone's cup of tea, but I love it. Maca has been described as a 'superfood' because it contains over twenty amino acids, vitamins B and C, and the minerals calcium, copper and magnesium.

'Cruciferous' is just a fancy word for plants that belong to the cabbage family. This one grows in the Andes of central Peru, in tough conditions and at very high altitudes — above 13 000 feet. It's associated with reduced anxiety and symptoms of depression.

There is growing evidence that the probiotics found in yoghurts with live, active cultures may help people cope with anxiety, stress and pain. In an amazing study in 2000 at Dartmouth Medical School, people with a history of brain injury were randomly assigned to one of three treatments: ingesting yoghurt in a medicine cup, taking a 5-minute tour of the facility, or music therapy for a 5-minute period. Interestingly, the group prescribed yoghurt recorded the most improvements in their cognitive functions.

Makes 1

¼ cup (20 g) rolled (traditional) oats
¼ cup (40 g) almonds (or any other nut you like)
½–1 cup (125–250 ml) liquid (water or your choice of milk: dairy, rice, oat, soy, coconut, almond)

1 frozen banana, chopped (fresh is also good)
1–2 teaspoons maca powder (optional)
¼ teaspoon ground cinnamon
pinch of ground nutmeg

1. Put all ingredients into a blender and blend until smooth.

TIP: 1–2 pitted medjool dates, extra rolled oats or a dollop of natural yoghurt will all make the consistency thicker and more substantial, so can be added as optional extras.

I PINE FOR YOU

dairy-free / egg-free / gluten-free /
grain-free / nut-free / wheat-free

Pineapple always puts me in a good mood – probably
because I feel like I'm in a tropical paradise when I eat
it. But seriously, pineapples are so good for you: they're
packed full of fibre, vitamin C, antioxidants to help your
immune system run more optimally, and manganese,
which is essential for your body to produce energy.
In the core of the pineapple is a concentration of enzymes,
including bromelain, which can reduce inflammation,
swelling and the symptoms of chronic runny nose; helps
wounds to heal; and may alleviate symptoms of asthma.

Makes 1

1 cup (110 g) chopped fresh
    or frozen pineapple
1 cup (20 g) baby spinach
    leaves
½ avocado, peeled
finely grated zest and
    juice of 1 lime

1 cup (250 ml)
    coconut water
small handful (¼ cup)
    mint leaves
small handful (¼ cup)
    ice cubes

One of my faves – did you
know that coconut water
is naturally free of fat and
cholesterol, AND that 1 cup
has more potassium than
a banana? Not to mention
being super hydrating.

1. Put all ingredients into a blender and blend until smooth.

TIP: For a more substantial smoothie, add 1 frozen
banana and ½ cup (125 ml) coconut milk (canned
variety). My son Harvey calls this version the 'super
power' blend.

RASPBERRY CHIA

dairy-free / egg-free / gluten-free /
grain-free / nut-free / wheat-free

Flip, did you know that they also have a high concentration of ellagic acid, a phenolic compound that appears to slow the growth of cancer cells?[19] A truly smart snack.

As a kid, I loved raspberry split ice-creams so they are the inspiration for this smoothie. Raspberries are not only delicious, but nutritious – they contain loads of vitamin C and are believed to have the highest concentration of antioxidants amongst all fruits.

Makes 1

1 cup (150 g) frozen
  raspberries
½ cup (125 ml) canned
  coconut milk

½ cup (125 ml) cold water
1–2 teaspoons chia seeds

1. Put all ingredients into a blender and blend until smooth. Let the smoothie stand for 5–10 minutes so the chia seeds expand and thicken the smoothie.

One of the remarkable properties of chia is that it is hydrophilic (water-loving) and can absorb up to 10 times its weight – awesome!

CHOCONANA

dairy-free (option) / egg-free / gluten-free / grain-free / wheat-free

Just like a chocolate milkshake . . . only packed full of nutrients! Use two bananas for a super-thick, substantial smoothie – otherwise one is fine. Likewise, the ground linseeds will make this extra thick and add a great nutritional boost.

Makes 1

1–2 frozen bananas, chopped
1–2 pitted medjool dates
¼ cup (40 g) raw unsalted cashews (or you can use almonds, hazelnuts or macadamia nuts)
2 tablespoons cacao powder
1 teaspoon ground cinnamon
1 tablespoon ground linseeds (optional)
1 cup (250 ml) water or your choice of milk

1. Put all ingredients into a blender and blend until smooth.

Linseeds, also known as flaxseeds, are little nutritional powerhouses. They come in Hawthorn Football Club colours – brown and golden – and both kinds score the same nutritional goals. Linseeds are high in omega-3 fats, which play a role in maintaining normal cholesterol levels.

ZUCCHINI AND KEFIR

dairy-free (option) / egg-free / gluten-free /
grain-free / nut-free / wheat-free

This smoothie is more savoury than sweet so it's not for everyone, but kefir is great for gut health because it contains live probiotics. In other words, 'good' or 'helpful' bacteria which can help keep the gut healthy. If you are new to kefir, which is a cultured, fermented drink with a tart taste and fizzy texture, start with a small amount and slowly increase it over a few weeks. Originally from the mountainous region known as the Caucasus, between the Black and Caspian Seas in Eastern Europe, it's made with kefir 'grains'. There are a few different brands of kefir (including some Australian ones) which can be made from milk, coconut and rice – experiment and see what you like best. Just remember to read the label so you know what you are getting.

Makes 1

One of my favourite smart snacks, pumpkin seeds or pepitas are a rich source of tryptophan, an amino acid (protein building block) that your body converts into serotonin, which in turn is converted into melatonin, the 'sleep hormone'. Good news for sleep and mood!

Flip, did you know that 1 cup of chopped parsley provides over 1000 per cent of an individual's daily recommended vitamin K intake? Incredible. Vitamin K, so named because it comes from the German word *koagulation*, is a fat-soluble vitamin that plays a vital role in healthy blood clot formation. It also promotes bone density.

2 cups (200 g) chopped zucchini (courgette)
½ cup (125 g) plain kefir
½ cup (125 ml) water
1 tablespoon pumpkin seeds (optional)

small handful (¼ cup) flat-leaf parsley leaves (optional)
pinch of sea salt

1. Put all ingredients into a blender and blend until smooth.

TIP: To make this drink dairy-free, choose a coconut or rice kefir instead of one that's milk-based.

MANGO LASSI

egg-free / gluten-free / grain-free /
nut-free / wheat-free

Channel your Indian deity and get divine with this
smoothie! When travelling in India, I loved trying
all the different lassis (a popular traditional yoghurt-
based drink) on offer in each town or village.
I prefer to use frozen mango as it gives the lassi
a very thick and creamy taste and texture,
but fresh mango works well too.

Makes 1

½ cup (140 g)
   Greek-style yoghurt
½ cup (125 ml) water or
   ice cubes
1 cup (110 g) chopped fresh
   or frozen mango
pinch of ground nutmeg

pinch of ground cinnamon
   (optional)
1 teaspoon rosewater
   (optional)

1. Put all ingredients into a blender and blend until smooth.

**TIP: For something a little more exotic, try a sprinkling
of cardamom and a splash of rosewater.**

Originating in India, Nepal
and Bhutan, cardamom may
have some anti-depressant
properties (however further
research is required). It gets the
bronze medal when it comes to
expensive spices – gold going
to saffron and silver to vanilla.[20]

IT'S EASY BEING GREEN

dairy-free / egg-free / gluten-free /
grain-free / nut-free / wheat-free

I reckon green smoothies are the first step in solving any
and every problem! They make you feel great, and then
because you feel great you can tackle problems or
view the world in a positive frame of mind. Trust me –
you never feel bad after a green smoothie.

Makes 1 large or 2 small

Also known as an alligator pear
or butter fruit – who knew?

Long endorsed as the food that
gave Popeye his ginormous
muscles and offers a trifecta
of goodies for enhancing
eye health: beta-carotene,
lutein and vitamin E!

½–1 avocado , peeled, stone
  removed
1 granny smith apple, cored,
  chopped
1 cup (20 g) baby spinach
  leaves

1 cup (100 g) chopped
  Lebanese cucumber
juice of 1 lemon
1–2 teaspoons matcha
  powder (optional)

1. Put all ingredients into a blender and blend until smooth.

TIP: Lebanese cucumbers are perfect for this recipe
as they have a thin skin and no seeds, but if you can't
find them then simply replace with the common
continental cucumber.

HIT THE TROPICS

dairy-free / egg-free / gluten-free /
grain-free / nut-free / wheat-free

Papaya is an excellent source of carotenoids, which help build your immunity. It is also full of fibre so it keeps you feeling fuller for longer and it assists your digestive system by breaking down foods – so, if you are feeling sluggish and bloated, try this tropical drink.

Makes 1 large or 2 small

1 cup (100 g) chopped papaya

1 cup (110 g) chopped pineapple

1 cup (250 ml) coconut water

squeeze of lime or lemon juice

handful (½ cup) mint leaves

small handful (¼ cup) ice cubes

And if all that's not enough reason to give it a go, what if I told you that just 1 cup of papaya contains double a child's daily recommended amount of vitamin C and a third of their daily vitamin A requirements? Papaya fruit has more vitamin C than an orange!

1. Put all ingredients into a blender and blend until smooth.

TUMMY TONIC

dairy-free / egg-free / gluten-free /
grain-free / nut-free / wheat-free

I don't usually recommend drinking juices because
the pulp has been removed – and with it the fibre,
which helps regulate blood sugars and the feeling of
being full. You lose out on some of the vitamins and
minerals, too. However, juices can have a place and this
one is a fantastic tonic for a tummy upset with nerves or
from eating too much of the wrong food. You can
also turn it into a wholefood smoothie: simply peel the
lemon, then toss all the ingredients into a blender,
blend on high for a minute or two, add 1 cup of water and
drink or strain through a sieve for a smoother texture.
If you don't have any lemons, use a lime.

Makes 1

2 packham pears, cored
2 cups (160 g) chopped
savoy cabbage
1 lemon, peeled and halved

2–3 slices fresh ginger,
peeled
small handful (¼ cup)
ice cubes, to serve

The vitamin K and plant
pigments in cabbage are
crucial for the production of
sphingolipids, found in the
myelin sheath around nerves
that protects them and enables
them to function properly.

1. Pass all the ingredients through a juicer. Serve over
ice cubes.

Hummus Balls (page 45), Zesty Coconut Balls (page 40) and Apricot Balls (page 41)

Chocolate Coconut Balls (page 48) and Matcha Balls (page 46)

Raspberry Chia Smoothie (page 58) and Mango Lassi (page 61)

Beet the Bloat (page 65) and It's Easy Being Green (page 62)

Green Pea Dip (page 78), Roasted Carrot Dip (page 74) and Gluten-Free Almond Meal Crackers (page 85)

Chocolate Dip (page 82)

Beetroot, Carrot and Parsnip Chips (page 91)

Sweet Potato Fries (page 94) and Zucchini Chips (page 95)

Roasted Veg Frittata (page 105)

Chocolate Mousse (page 103), Coconut Rice (page 107) and Perfect Parfait (page 104)

Make It a Date (page 117) and Banana Bites (page 121)

BEET THE BLOAT

dairy-free / egg-free / gluten-free /
grain-free / nut-free / wheat-free

Clever, I see what you did there! How about 'Flatulence Fighter'?

Air and energy get trapped in your tummy when you sit for ages, and when you're anxious you can get butterflies or knots in your tummy too. When this happens, a juice with beetroots, carrots and ginger is fantastic to beat the bloat.

As long as the butterflies are flying in formation, it is okay.

Makes 1

1 beetroot , washed to
   remove any dirt,
   stalks removed
1–2 carrots, ends removed

1 granny smith apple, cored
1–2 slices fresh ginger,
   peeled
water (optional)

Beetroot has been described as a health food titan: low in fat, full of vitamins and minerals, and packed with powerful antioxidants. A study at Wake Forest University, North Carolina, tracked adults with hypertension and discovered that those who consumed beetroot juice as well as exercising showed brain connectivity that had increased to a level usually seen in younger adults![21]

1. Chop the beetroot, carrots and apple..
2. Pass all the ingredients through a juicer. Add enough water to reach desired consistency. You can adjust the volumes of the different ingredients to achieve the perfect taste for you. For younger kids who may not like the earthy flavour of the beetroot, amp up the ratio of carrots and use a sweet apple, such as royal gala or fuji.

TIP: If you don't have a juicer, blend all the ingredients in a high-powered blender, then strain the mixture through a fine sieve, using a wooden spoon or spatula to extract every drop! It is a bit messy and takes a bit longer but it's worth it.

GET RED(DY) AND GO

dairy-free / egg-free / gluten-free /
grain-free / nut-free / wheat-free

I call this the Get Reddy and Go juice because it's bright red and you'll be set to go once you've had it!

Makes 1

The brain depends on essential vitamins and minerals to function. By any measures of nutrient density, kale gets a top place on the podium because just 1 cup of raw kale delivers a huge dose of vitamins C, A and K.

2 cups chopped kale or
   spinach leaves
1 lemon, peeled and halved
1 beetroot, washed, stalks
   removed

1 Lebanese cucumber
1 green apple, cored
large handful (1 cup) ice
   cubes, to serve

1. Chop the fruit and vegetables into pieces.
2. Pass all the ingredients through a juicer. Serve over ice cubes.

KOMBUCHA 'JUICE'

dairy-free / egg-free / gluten-free /
grain-free / nut-free / wheat-free

Like kefir, kombucha is fermented and has a
bit of a fizzy, funny taste, so if you are new to
this drink, just start with small amounts until you
get used to it because the benefits are fantastic.

Makes 1

1 granny smith apple, cored
½ cup (10 g) baby spinach
  leaves
½ cup (50 g) chopped
  Lebanese or continental
  cucumber

1 cup (250 ml) kombucha
  (or do half and half with
  soda water)
small handful (1/4 cup)
  mint leaves

Traditionally made by
fermenting sweetened tea with
what's referred to as a SCOBY,
kombucha contains a large
number of healthy bacteria
known as probiotics which line
your digestive tract and may
support your mental health.

1. Chop the fruit and vegetables into pieces.
2. Pass all the ingredients through a juicer.

RECIPE LIST

HUMMUS IN A HURRY

SIMPLE GUACAMOLE

ROASTED CARROT DIP

TZATZIKI

CORN SALSA

TOMATO SALSA

GREEN PEA DIP

SPINACH AND RICOTTA DIP

SATAY DIP

TAPENADE

CHOCOLATE DIP

FLATBREAD CRACKERS

BAGEL CRACKERS

GLUTEN-FREE ALMOND MEAL CRACKERS

3

DIPS

TO DIG INTO

So true, Flip. A recent study suggests that these emulsifiers – detergent-like food additives found in a variety of processed foods – have the potential to damage the intestinal barrier, leading to inflammation and increasing our risk of chronic disease.

MANY COMMERCIALLY PRODUCED DIPS are fatty, oily and full of stabilisers, thickeners and other things that are hard to spell . Not very appetising! Homemade dips, on the other hand, can be packed full of nutritional goodness and make a really delicious smart snack. Most dip recipes need just a few key ingredients and can easily be adjusted to suit your family's taste buds. And almost anything can be turned into a dip!

Another thing to love about dips is that they are quick and easy to make and you really can't go wrong because they don't rely on cooking times and temperatures. For this reason dips are a great introduction to food preparation for kids who are new to the kitchen and cooking. If your kids are old enough to use a food processor or stick blender safely then they could make many of these recipes themselves or with you for a shared experience.

Dips also keep well in the fridge, so make a big batch, divide into separate containers, and you will have afternoon tea sorted for a few days.

Bagel chips (baked, not fried) are healthier than a regular potato chip, with 60 per cent less fat. They're also free from artificial colours, flavours, preservatives, cholesterol, added MSG, fake tans or any other nasties!

Mother Nature made the best dippers in raw carrots, cucumbers, celery, snow peas, sugar peas, red capsicums and mushrooms, as well as lightly steamed beans and cauliflower florets. Homemade Flatbread Crackers (see recipe page 83) or Bagel Crackers (see recipe page 84) add another kind of crunch.

Homemade crackers can be made easily with a yeast-free or unleavened bread like mountain, sorj or khobz. All of these breads have a wonderful history and herald from the Middle East. I love that these recipes have barely changed over thousands of years – anything that's lasted that long has to be good! Alternatively, there are plenty of delicious wholegrain, corn, quinoa and rice crackers available in supermarkets these days as well as raw seed crackers in delis and specialty stores.

It's easy to get carried away with the amount of bread or crackers eaten with these dips. To help avoid this happening, I always put one part bread or crackers to four parts veggies when making a dip platter.

A.K.A. the Flip Dip Formula!

And if you're still in need of dipper inspiration, look no further than the next chapter: chips! (See page 78.)

Finally, a note on chilli, which can be a lovely addition to the corn salsa, tomato salsa, guacamole and satay dips in this chapter. There are many kinds of chilli, from those with sweet, smoky and spicy flavours, to the mild and medium, all the way to head-spinning lip-numbing hot. If you want more information, why not check out the Scoville scale which ranks them from around the world according to their heat and intensity. This is useful if you are wanting to introduce new flavours to younger kids. If handling the seeds of the hot chillies, please wash your hands before touching your eyes, lips or face, as the heat can transfer to your soft fleshy skin and cause considerable pain.

HUMMUS IN A HURRY

dairy-free / egg-free / gluten-free /
grain-free / nut-free / wheat-free

Hummus is also low in saturated fat and offers complex carbohydrates, great for making hungry kids feel satisfied and full.

Also known as garbanzo beans, chickpeas are one of the best sources of magnesium, making them a premier brain-boosting food. Magnesium maintains healthy brain function, can improve sleep quality, and may help reduce the symptoms of depression, too.

Hummus , made with chickpeas and tahini, is a great source of plant-based protein. I adore chickpeas because they are so versatile (and nutritious) – so I always have a tin in the cupboard! They are an excellent source of essential nutrients, iron, folate, phosphorus and fibre. Did you know Australia is the second biggest producer of chickpeas after India?

Makes about 2 cups

400 g tin chickpeas, rinsed, drained
¼ cup (60 g) tahini (at room temperature)
1–2 cloves garlic, chopped
2 tablespoons olive oil
finely grated zest and juice of 1 lemon

sea salt and ground black pepper
small handful fresh flat-leaf parsley, chopped
¼ teaspoon smoked paprika (optional)
¼ teaspoon ground cumin (optional)

1. Put the chickpeas, tahini, garlic, olive oil, lemon juice and zest and parsley into a food processor and process until smooth. If it's too thick, add a little more olive oil or water.
2. Season with salt and pepper. Add smoked paprika and ground cumin, if using.

Great idea!

TIP: You can replace some or all of the tahini with a few round slices of banana for a sweeter tasting dip which is always a big hit with younger kids.

SIMPLE GUACAMOLE

dairy-free / egg-free / gluten-free /
grain-free / nut-free / wheat-free

Aussies adore avocados and we have doubled our
consumption since 2007 to an average of 4 kg
per person, per year. I reckon I eat 20 kg a year!
Thanks to their creamy taste and smooth texture,
avos go perfectly in salads, on toast, in smoothies and
of course as guacamole! (They make a great dessert too,
so check out my recipe for Chocolate Mousse, page 103).
Avocados are a nutrient-dense food containing
20 vitamins and minerals , and virtually the only fruit
that contains monounsaturated fat – good fat!

Makes about 1½ cups

1 large avocado
finely grated zest of
  ½ lemon
2 tablespoons lemon juice
2 tablespoons olive oil

handful (½ cup) coriander
  leaves and stems, washed
sea salt and ground black
  pepper, to taste

At the risk of having an
explosion in an avocado fact
factory, did you know that
while we usually associate
potassium with bananas,
a single avocado delivers
twice as much of this
essential mineral?

1. *Carefully* remove the skin and stone from the avocado
   (don't let the little ones near this task!).
2. Put the avocado, lemon zest, lemon juice, olive oil,
   coriander leaves and stems into a food processor
   and process until smooth.
3. Season to taste with salt and pepper. Add more lemon
   juice or olive oil if required.

In the UK, the retailer Marks
and Spencer has launched
a stoneless avocado to help
prevent the increasingly
common avocado-induced
knife injury known by surgeons
as 'avocado hand'. Seriously!

**TIP: Add one chopped tomato with the seeds removed
and a *little* finely chopped fresh chilli or a light sprinkling
of ground chilli powder for some spice.**

ROASTED CARROT DIP

dairy-free / egg-free / gluten-free /
grain-free / nut-free / wheat-free

Carrots are an excellent source of beta-carotene. The clever human body turns beta-carotene into vitamin A, which is brilliant for eyesight, skin health, and normal growth.

It's worth the effort of roasting the carrots for their gorgeous sweet flavour! The fresh ginger and ground turmeric add extra healthy elements to this dip because – if memory serves me correctly – they have both been found to be good for assisting memory!

Makes about 2½ cups

1 tablespoon olive or
   coconut oil
1 teaspoon ground cumin
1 teaspoon ground turmeric
sea salt and ground
   black pepper

1 kg (about 10) carrots,
   peeled and cut into
   even 2 cm rounds
2–4 cloves garlic, peeled
   (optional)
2 knobs fresh ginger, peeled
   and grated (or 1 teaspoon
   ground ginger)

The sulfur-containing compounds in garlic are a brilliant source of antioxidants and anti-inflammatories. Historians say that Egyptian pharaohs plied their pyramid-builders with garlic for strength – so work like an Egyptian!

1. Preheat the oven to 180°C. Line a large baking tray with baking paper.
2. Combine the oil, cumin, turmeric and a pinch of salt and pepper in a large bowl. Add the carrots, garlic and ginger to the bowl and stir until evenly coated with spices.
3. Spread carrots over the lined tray and bake for 30–40 minutes or until tender. (After 15 minutes shake the tray to ensure the veggies are not sticking and check that the garlic and ginger aren't browning. Remove if they are. You want them to be softened but not brown.)
4. Allow to cool slightly, then transfer to a food processor and process until smooth. Season with extra salt and pepper.

TZATZIKI

egg-free / gluten-free / grain-free /
nut-free / wheat-free

This is a delicious dip: refreshing when served chilled and nutritious thanks to the probiotics in the yoghurt, which are good for gut health. Just beware – there's real yoghurt and then there's confectionary 'yoghurt'. Try to avoid any no- or low-fat yoghurts as these are full of sugars and other things to bulk them up and improve the taste. Yoghurt is a fermented product so it should taste a little zingy but many commercially produced yoghurts (especially those marketed at kids) have sugars or flavours added to disguise this taste. If you want to know *exactly* what's in your yoghurt, you can make your own at home – it's a really fun foodie experiment for the kids to try.

This brilliant Greek concoction is sky-high in calcium, fat, sodium, protein and vitamin K, plus lots of other vitamins and minerals – brain nirvana!

Good-quality yoghurt contains excellent levels of lactic acid that promote healthy skin. In India, it's long been used as a moisturiser to revitalise dull, dry skin.

Makes about 2½ cups

2 cups (550 g) Greek-style
   yoghurt
2–6 cloves garlic, finely
   grated (this depends on
   how much you love garlic,
   how large the cloves are,
   how potent they are . . .
   and how Greek you are!)

½ continental cucumber,
   peeled, deseeded and
   finely chopped
1 teaspoon sea salt
1 tablespoon lemon juice
2–3 mint leaves, finely
   chopped

1. Put all the ingredients into a large bowl and stir well.
2. Cover and place in the fridge to chill for about 30 minutes, to allow flavours to develop before serving.

TIP: Tzatziki and Roasted Carrot Dip (opposite) will keep for up to 3 days in an airtight container in the fridge.

CORN SALSA

dairy-free / egg-free / gluten-free /
grain-free / nut-free / wheat-free

Flip, did you know that 'salsa'
is the Spanish word for sauce?

Red onions have great levels of
sulfur that can boost the amino
acid components that help the
body to function optimally.

I love making this salsa as it's easy to change the recipe according to the ingredients on hand, like adding some finely chopped red onion or red capsicum, or a deseeded tomato. The mint and coriander combo is fabulous but you can use one or the other if you prefer. This salsa works really well with corn chips or corn crackers. Pour leftovers onto a salad like a dressing, dollop it on top of cooked porridge or just eat it with a spoon like my son Harvey does!

Makes 3 cups

2 cups (320 g) fresh corn
  kernels (frozen also works
  and canned is okay)
1 mango, chopped
  (about 1 cup)
finely grated zest and
  juice of 1 lime
small handful (¼ cup)
  coriander leaves, chopped

small handful (¼ cup)
  mint leaves, chopped
pinch of ground chilli
  powder (optional – and
  always add very carefully
  and in small amounts!)
sea salt and ground black
  pepper

1. Bring a medium saucepan of water to the boil. Add the corn and cook for 1–2 minutes or until tender. Drain and refresh with cold water to stop the cooking process. Drain.
2. Process the mango in a food processor (or blender) until smooth. Transfer to a large bowl. Stir in corn, lime zest, juice, coriander, mint and chilli (if using), then season.
3. Cover and place in the fridge to chill for at least 30 minutes to allow the flavours to develop.

TOMATO SALSA

dairy-free / egg-free / gluten-free /
grain-free / nut-free / wheat-free

This tasty dip can be made either hot and spicy with
some chilli or mild and fresh with lots of coriander.
Serve with crunchy celery sticks – their shape makes
it easy to scoop up lots of dip. It's also fabulous served
with corn chips – just read the nutritional label on the
packet to make sure the hungry hordes won't be eating
loads of hidden fats and sugars.

Makes about 2 cups

1 tablespoon olive oil
½ red onion, finely chopped
1 clove garlic, finely
  chopped
¼–1 teaspoon dried
  chilli flakes , to taste

4 tomatoes, finely diced
small handful (¼ cup)
  basil or flat-leaf parsley
  leaves, chopped
sea salt and ground
  black pepper

As well as adding a fiery kick,
chilli flakes have a good dose
of vitamin A, a nutrient that
helps keep the immune
system healthy.

1. Heat the olive oil in a heavy-based saucepan over medium
   heat. Add the onion, garlic and chilli and cook, stirring
   often, for 5 minutes or until softened but not browned.

2. Add the tomatoes and bring to the boil, then reduce the
   heat and hold at a gentle simmer for 10 minutes or until
   thick. Stir in the basil or parsley and season with plenty
   of salt and pepper.

3. If you want a smooth dip, cool slightly then process in a
   food processor or blender, otherwise leave it a bit chunky.
   Allow to cool before serving.

**TIP: Tomato Salsa and Corn Salsa (opposite) will keep
for up to 3 days in an airtight container in the fridge.**

GREEN PEA DIP
(A.K.A. DIPPY)

dairy-free / egg-free / gluten-free /
grain-free / wheat-free

Frozen pea packets aren't just for sprained ankles and headaches; they are also perfect to make this dip. I always have a packet of frozen peas (and corn) on hand so that this dip can be whipped up in minutes. There is nothing, however, like the taste of fresh peas, so get the kids on shelling duty! When the brain is racing, doing something simple with your hands can be calming – a great antidote for stressed students. Finally: don't skimp on the mint as it elevates the dip to another level.

Makes about 2½ cups

Who knew that unassuming green peas are packed with manganese, iron, protein and dietary fibre? Plus the nutrients in peas make a range of brain chemicals, including neurotransmitters – now that's smart!

2 cups (220 g) frozen peas
  (or can use fresh)
large handful (1 cup)
  mint leaves
½ cup (70 g) pine nuts
  (or blanched almonds)

finely grated zest of 1 lemon
  (adjust to taste)
2 tablespoons lemon juice
1–2 tablespoons olive or
  coconut oil
sea salt and ground
  black pepper

1. Bring a medium saucepan of water to the boil over high heat. Add the peas and cook for 3 minutes or until just tender: you don't want them super-mushy. Drain.
2. Put peas into a food processor with mint, pine nuts, lemon zest and juice, and 1 tablespoon of the oil and process until smooth-ish. I like it to be a little chunky. If you want a smooth consistency, add a little more oil or water. Season to taste with salt and pepper.

SPINACH AND RICOTTA DIP

egg-free / gluten-free / grain-free /
nut-free / wheat-free

I love the simplicity and lightness of this dip – plus it packs a nutritional punch. As well as being teamed with your child's dipper of choice, it's lovely dolloped on a roasted potato or spread on bread instead of mayo or butter. For something different, you can replace the ricotta cheese with ½ cup of cashews which have been soaked in boiling water for half an hour, then drained. It's always good to include a splash of lemon juice when eating spinach as it helps the absorption of the iron.

Makes about 2 cups

200 g baby spinach leaves
½ cup (65 g) smooth
  ricotta cheese

finely grated zest of 1 lemon
  (optional)
sea salt and ground
  black pepper

Flip, did you know that cashews are actually the kidney-shaped seeds at the bottom of the cashew apple, the fruit of the cashew tree? They are a tiny parcel of iron, magnesium, vitamin B6, protein and important amino acids, which may be of some benefit for those with mild depression and anxiety!

1. Bring a medium saucepan of water to the boil over high heat. Add the spinach and blanch for 1 minute or until bright green. Drain and refresh with cold water to stop the cooking process. Drain well.
2. Squeeze excess liquid out of the spinach. Put spinach, ricotta and lemon zest (if using) into a food processor and process until the desired consistency is reached – either chunky or smooth! Season with salt and pepper. For more creaminess, add another dollop of ricotta.

TIP: Spinach and Ricotta Dip and Green Pea Dip (opposite) will keep for up to 3 days in an airtight container in the fridge.

SATAY DIP

dairy-free / egg-free / gluten-free /
grain-free / wheat-free

Excellent idea – tempeh is high in protein, probiotics and a wide array of vitamins and minerals.

This dip goes beautifully with strips of tempeh , red capsicums, lightly steamed cauliflower florets and green beans. Sometimes I add a ripe banana and some cinnamon for a delicious natural sweet twist, which is a winner with younger kids. I prefer the mild flavour of tamari over soy sauce, plus it's gluten-free, making it suitable for coeliacs.

Makes about 2 cups

1 tablespoon coconut oil
2 knobs fresh ginger, peeled
    and grated
1 clove garlic, grated
½–1 teaspoon dried chilli
    flakes (optional)
1 cup (280 g) peanut butter
    (or almond or any other
    nut butter)

1 cup (250 ml) canned
    coconut milk
2 tablespoons tamari
small handful (¼ cup)
    coriander leaves,
    chopped

Even a small dollop of almond butter contains a generous amount of magnesium, with the potential to boost heart health by promoting the flow of blood, oxygen and nutrients.

1. Heat the coconut oil in a small saucepan over low heat. Add the ginger, garlic and chilli (if using) and cook for 2–3 minutes, stirring often, until fragrant but not golden.
2. Add peanut butter, coconut milk and tamari, and hold at a gentle simmer for 5–10 minutes or until the sauce is thick. Stir in the coriander . Serve warm.

Got a kid who detests coriander? Medical studies have revealed that the genetic constitution of an individual determines whether they will love or loathe its taste – so the protests are probably real!

TIP: Satay Dip will keep for up to 3 days in an airtight container in the fridge.

TAPENADE

dairy-free / egg-free / gluten-free /
grain-free / nut-free / wheat-free

If your child or teenager prefers salty things to sweet, this olive dip delivers in spades! It's best served with golden sourdough toast fingers, but it can also be stirred through pasta, dolloped on top of steamed veggies or spread on toast for breakfast instead of Vegemite. When making this tapenade, I add lots of fresh parsley – it not only gives it a flavour boost but it also has high levels of antioxidants, including vitamins A, C and K. Adding a mushroom beefs up the vitamin B, selenium and potassium content of the dip – and it knocks out a bit of the intensity of the olives and capers.

Makes about 1 cup

1 cup (150 g) pitted
    kalamata olives
1 tablespoon capers
1 tablespoon olive oil
2 tablespoons lemon juice
    or white wine vinegar

finely grated zest of 1 lemon
small handful (¼ cup)
    flat-leaf parsley leaves
1 large mushroom, chopped
    (optional)
ground black pepper

1. Rinse the olives and capers to remove the excess brine.

2. Put olives, capers, olive oil, lemon juice and zest, parsley and mushroom (if using) into a food processor and process until smooth. Season with several grinds of pepper to taste.

TIP: Tapenade will keep for up to 1 week in an airtight container in the fridge.

It's also an excellent source of folate and iron, Flip!

Here's a creepy fact: did you know that mushrooms are more closely related in DNA to humans than to plants? Like human skin, they can produce vitamin D by being exposed to sunlight. If you expose a freshly cut shiitake mushroom to the sun for 8 hours, gills up, you can multiply its vitamin D content by as much as 4600 times – no shiitake!

CHOCOLATE DIP

dairy-free / egg-free / gluten-free /
grain-free / nut-free / wheat-free

For something a little sweet but still healthy,
this dip is perfect. Instead of veggie dippers, though,
use fruits like strawberries, chopped green apple,
honeydew melon, cantaloupe , pineapple
or perhaps a few dried apricots.

Cantaloupes are packed with vitamin A and beta-carotene, plus lutein, zeaxanthin and cryptoxanthin – a trio of powerful antioxidants that help protect the macular region of the eye.

Makes about 1 cup

¼ cup (25 g) cacao powder
¼ cup (60 g) coconut oil, melted
¼ cup (60 g) tahini (at room temperature)
½ teaspoon ground cinnamon
1 tablespoon maple syrup or honey

1 teaspoon maca powder (optional)
extra coconut milk or oil (to thin the dip)
½ ripe banana (to thicken the dip)

Honey boosts brain function by helping your body absorb calcium. It takes 500 honey bees 4 weeks to make 1 kg of honey, all working together seamlessly in the hive.

1. Put the cacao powder, coconut oil, tahini, cinnamon, maple syrup and maca powder (if using) into a food processor and process until smooth.
2. Adjust with either extra coconut milk or oil to thin the dip or half a ripe banana to thicken it. Experiment with the consistency and flavour.

TIP: Chocolate Dip will keep for 3–5 days in an airtight container in the fridge.

FLATBREAD CRACKERS

dairy-free / egg-free / nut-free

Unleavened mountain bread and sorj bread are perfect for
making wholemeal flatbread crackers quickly and easily.
Pita bread can also be used for this recipe by carefully
separating the two sides of the pocket – so one packet
goes a long way. Because mountain bread is thin it defrosts
quickly, so I always keep a packet handy in the freezer
so I can whip up a pizza, wrap or crackers on the fly.
(See note on page 21, about freezing bread.)

Makes 2 slices

1 tablespoon olive oil
1 clove garlic, grated
sea salt and ground
   black pepper

2 slices any 'flat' bread
   (such as mountain,
   sorj, pita)

A truly wondrous substance,
olive oil contains many
antioxidants including
vitamin E, carotenoids
and oleuropein.

1. Combine the olive oil, garlic and salt and pepper to taste
   in a small bowl. Brush the flatbread evenly with the olive
   oil mixture.
2. Preheat the grill on high. Grill the bread for 1–2 minutes
   or until golden and crisp. Alternatively you can microwave
   each slice individually on HIGH (100 per cent) for
   45 seconds–1 minute (depending on your microwave).
   Allow to stand for 30 seconds to cool and stiffen.
3. Break bread up into bite-sized pieces.

**TIP: Flatbread Crackers will keep for up to 1 week in an
airtight container. I always choose an Australian brand
of olive oil as I've found the quality to be the best in
the world!**

BAGEL CRACKERS

dairy-free / egg-free / nut-free

If there is one food that transcends countries, cultures and kitchens, it would have to be bagels! From the crunchy caramel-coloured crust to the chewy, doughy centre, they're delicious, but they are made with a high-gluten flour, are often large and don't contain much nutritional value. Bagel chips are a modern invention and store-bought ones can be very high in fat and salt, but making your own is easy, and just one bagel sliced thinly goes a long way on a platter with dips and veggies.

Makes 16–20

Did you know that bagels are the only type of bread that is boiled before being baked? After the dough is shaped into a circle, they are dunked in boiling water for 3–5 minutes on each side, drained and then baked for about 10 minutes. Given that one bagel equals more than 3 slices of bread in terms of carbohydrates, you might like to try brown or wholemeal bagels for added nutrients.

1 **bagel**
olive oil (optional)

salt and ground black pepper (optional)

1. Using a serrated knife, carefully slice the bagel horizontally into 1 cm-thick rounds. Toast in a toaster until golden, then allow to cool. Chop or break into pieces.

Or

1. Preheat the oven to 200°C. Line a baking tray with baking paper. Slice the bagel in half and place on the tray. Lightly brush with olive oil and season with salt and pepper.
2. Bake for 4 minutes until golden. Using tongs, turn slices over and lightly brush with a little more olive oil. Bake for a further 3–4 minutes or until golden. Cool then break into pieces to serve.

TIP: Bagel Crackers and Gluten-Free Almond Meal Crackers (opposite) will keep for up to 1 week in an airtight container.

GLUTEN-FREE ALMOND MEAL CRACKERS

gluten-free / grain-free / wheat-free

These crackers are gluten-free and made with almond meal and an egg, so they're full of good fats and protein.

Makes about 20

2 cups (240 g) ground
  almonds
1 egg

Flavouring options:
a few grinds of sea salt and
  ground black pepper
1 teaspoon dried rosemary,

½ teaspoon garlic flakes,
¼ teaspoon chilli powder
and 2 tablespoons grated
parmesan cheese
½ teaspoon onion flakes
1 teaspoon sesame seeds
  and 1 teaspoon poppy
  seeds

1. Preheat the oven to 150°C. Line a large baking tray with baking paper.
2. Put the ground almonds, egg and your flavouring of choice into a food processor or blender and pulse until the mixture becomes a crumbly dough, about 1 minute.
3. Transfer mixture to a large sheet of baking paper and press into a ball. Place another sheet of baking paper over the top and use a rolling pin to roll out the mixture until about 1 cm thick. Press any thinning edges back into the mixture to even the edges.
4. Use a pizza cutter to cut dough into 2 cm × 2 cm squares, or a cookie cutter to make different shapes. Place crackers on lined tray and sprinkle some additional seasoning on top for decoration. Bake for 12 minutes or until just golden.
5. Allow to cool on a wire rack before eating.

RECIPE LIST

AVOCADO CHIPS

BEETROOT, CARROT AND PARSNIP CHIPS

KALE CHIPS

POLENTA WEDGES

SWEET POTATO FRIES

ZUCCHINI CHIPS

SALT AND VINEGAR CHIPS

CAULIFLOWER BLISS BOMBS

4

CHIPS

AHOY

THANKS TO DOCUMENTARIES LIKE the McDonald's experiment *Super Size Me*, books like Eric Schlosser's *Fast Food Nation*, and awareness raised through many organisations including Australia's peak nutritional body, Nutrition Australia, we now know that deep-fried food is bad for our health because it's loaded with saturated and trans fats and has little nutritional value. Chips, wedges and fries have traditionally been made by deep-frying potatoes.

These days, though, creative cooking has changed our view of what constitutes the humble chip and we now see them made from a range of delicious ingredients, such as avocado or beetroot, each one offering differing tastes and textures. Better still, rather than being an unhealthy snack, the modern chip can actually contribute to your child's day in a nutritious way.

So, ditch the deep fryer, grab some baking trays and turn on the oven to make these delicious alternatives to the old-school fried chip. Baking intensifies the flavours of the veggies because it reduces their water content, which is why baked chips are so tasty.

These chips are best eaten at the time of cooking, warm from the oven – just watch the roof of your mouth. Serve them for afternoon tea in a big bowl in the centre of the table for everyone to tuck into. Alternatively, grab some colourful containers like popcorn tubs or Chinese takeaway-style containers (both of which are available at the supermarket or $2 shops), and create individual serves for an after-dinner at-home movie night, or wrap them in a few layers of greaseproof paper to recreate the look of the traditional takeaway 'minimum chips' order.

If you are serving these chips to the kids with store-bought condiments like tomato sauce, sweet chilli sauce, mayonnaise or salsa, just remember to read the labels to check that they don't contain any cheap additives or fillers – or loads of sugar.

If you do still have a hankering for classic potato fries or wedges, here's my baked potato wedge recipe. I generally use a medium (200 g) potato per person and a 'floury' variety like the red-skinned, yellow-fleshed desiree because it has a thin skin. The russet burbank variety also works well because it is large, so you can get lots of good finger-sized fries from each spud. You'll find lots of good 'all-rounder' potatoes at supermarkets and markets that are fine to use too.

1. Preheat the oven to 200°C.
2. Cut your washed (but not peeled) potato into wedges of similar sizes (the size and thickness is your personal choice).
3. Put wedges in a large bowl, drizzle with a little olive oil and season with salt, pepper and any herbs and spices you like – perhaps a little sprinkling of chilli powder, smoked paprika or dried rosemary. Stir so the wedges are evenly coated.
4. Place wedges on a lined baking tray and cook in the oven for 20 minutes. Turn and continue to cook for another 10 minutes. Continue to turn the wedges every 10 minutes until they are golden and cooked through (which you can test with a skewer), approximately 40 minutes in total.
5. Transfer wedges to a serving dish, season with salt and pepper, and eat!

AVOCADO CHIPS

dairy-free / gluten-free (option) / nut-free

We mash it, we smash it, we can make a face mask with it . . . so why not create a chip with it? Avocados are high in fibre and healthy monounsaturated fats and make a lovely, delicate baked chip. To make this a gluten-free option, use gluten-free breadcrumbs.

Makes 8

Rice flour contains choline, which not only helps to transport cholesterol and triglycerides from the liver to where they're needed within the body, but is also a building block of the neurotransmitter acetylcholine, essential to good brain functioning.

Cayenne pepper contains vitamins B6, C and E, plus potassium and manganese. There are also flavonoids in it, which provide its powerful antioxidant properties.

1 firm avocado
1 egg
¼ cup (40 g) rice flour
1 cup (70 g) stale white
    breadcrumbs (see Tip)

sea salt and ground
    black pepper
¼–½ teaspoon cayenne
    pepper (optional)
lime juice, to serve

1. Preheat the oven to 220°C. Line a baking tray with baking paper.
2. Halve the avocado, remove the stone and peel away the skin. Cut the avocado into eight wedges.
3. Crack the egg into a shallow bowl and lightly whisk. Place the flour and breadcrumbs in two separate shallow bowls. Season breadcrumbs with salt and pepper and cayenne for some kick!
4. Working one at a time, dust each piece of avocado in the flour, then coat in the egg, allowing any excess to drip off. Place into the breadcrumb mixture until evenly coated.
5. Spread over the lined tray and bake for 10–15 minutes or until golden and crisp. Serve drizzled with lime juice.

TIP: For this dish, I use a white bread: even though I stick to wholemeal for almost everything else.

BEETROOT, CARROT AND PARSNIP CHIPS

dairy-free / egg-free / gluten-free /
grain-free / nut-free / wheat-free

The colourful combination of these chips looks appealing in a bowl and the flavours are delicious. While this recipe suggests making the chips using a mandolin (a kitchen utensil that cuts veggies evenly), if you don't have one these veggies also work well chopped into wedges.

Makes about 20
(depending on how big your veggies are!)

1 large beetroot
1 large carrot
1 large parsnip
2 tablespoons olive oil

sea salt and ground black
  pepper
2 teaspoons dried rosemary
  (optional)

1. Preheat the oven to 180°C. Line two baking trays with baking paper.
2. Wash and dry the veggies (don't worry about peeling). Cut them into rounds, about 1 cm thick. I use a mandolin to ensure they are the same thickness and cook evenly.
3. Spread veggie rounds on the lined trays. Lightly brush with the olive oil, season with salt and pepper, and sprinkle with rosemary (if using).
4. Bake for 20 minutes, then using tongs, turn the veggies and cook for 10 minutes further or until golden and crisp.
5. Set aside to cool a little before transferring to a big bowl in the centre of the table.
6. Serve warm or cold.

Let me tell you about Acciaroli, a little town in Italy where more than 10 per cent of the population of 700 people are over 100 years old. Unsurprisingly, it's been researched to discover the factors that contribute to its residents' longevity. The centenarians of Acciaroli are also known to have very low rates of heart disease and Alzheimer's disease due to unusually good blood circulation – and guess what? They put rosemary on everything!

KALE CHIPS

dairy-free / egg-free / gluten-free /
grain-free / nut-free / wheat-free

Kale is a long-leafed green or purple cabbage. It's best not eaten raw as it has some hard-to-digest components, especially for younger tummies, so blanch, juice or bake it instead. Kale is high in fibre, vitamins A, C and K, and folate, so it's a fantastic veggie to get into your child's day.

Makes about 30

1 bunch curly or flat kale
1–2 tablespoons coconut oil, melted
sea salt and ground black pepper
¼ teaspoon dried chilli flakes (optional)

½ teaspoon dried garlic flakes (optional)
½ teaspoon dried parsley flakes (optional)

1. Preheat the oven to 120°C. Line two baking trays with baking paper.
2. Tear the kale leaves into bite-sized pieces and discard the thick stalks .
3. Put kale and coconut oil into a large bowl. Using your hands, massage the oil into the leaves until evenly coated. Season with salt and pepper. Add any additional seasoning you like – chilli flakes, garlic flakes and dried parsley all work really well.
4. Spread kale evenly over the lined trays and bake for 10 minutes. Turn and cook for a further 10 minutes or until crisp. Serve.

No, no, no – that's wasteful, Flip! Turn those kale stems into a flavourful sauce to toss with pasta, dress your veggies or spread on sandwiches. Start by blanching the stems and then pick your favourite pesto recipe and get blending!

POLENTA WEDGES

egg-free / gluten-free /
nut-free / wheat-free

Polenta is milled from corn and carries flavours well,
so consider adding some other ingredients like peas,
chopped red capsicum or caramelised onion to mix things
up. There are three parts to making these wedges, all
straightforward, but allow about 75 minutes from start to
finish. You can cook the polenta and keep it in the fridge
in the tray for up to 2 days before making the wedges.

Polenta is a stellar source
of carotenoid, thought to
decrease the risk of certain
diseases, such as some
types of eye conditions.

Makes 12–15

1 cup (170 g) polenta
½ cup (30 g) grated
  parmesan cheese

sea salt and ground
  black pepper

1. Line a 16 cm × 26 cm (base measurement) roasting tin
   with baking paper.
2. Cook the polenta following packet instructions. Remove
   from the heat, add parmesan and stir until well combined.
   Pour polenta mixture into the prepared tin and smooth
   the surface with the back of a spoon. Set aside to cool.
3. Preheat the oven to 200°C. Line a large baking tray with
   baking paper. Turn the polenta slab out onto a clean
   work surface and cut into even-sized wedges, about
   7 cm long × 2 cm deep × 3 cm wide.
4. Place wedges on the lined tray and season well with
   salt and pepper (or any other spices you like). Bake for
   20 minutes, turning halfway through the cooking time,
   or until golden and crisp. Serve.

SWEET POTATO FRIES

dairy-free / egg-free / gluten-free /
grain-free / nut-free / wheat-free

Sweet potatoes are a nutritional powerhouse. They're an outstanding source of beta-carotene (precursor to vitamin A) and a good source of B1, B2, B6, C, manganese, copper, potassium, dietary fibre, niacin and phosphorus.

Lots of kids love sweet potatoes because, as their name suggests, they have a naturally sweet flavour. Once roasted, these sweet potato fries are even sweeter. I generally allow one sweet potato per person but you can adjust this to suit the size of the appetites you're cooking for.

Makes 5–10

Leave the skin on the sweet potato, because it's a great source of added fibre.

1 sweet potato
(about 200 g)
1 tablespoon coconut oil, melted

½–1 teaspoon ground cinnamon
sea salt

1. Preheat the oven to 200°C. Line a baking tray with baking paper.
2. Wash the potato and pat dry with absorbent paper (don't peel unless you want to). Cut the potato into fries, about 5 cm long × 1 cm wide × 1 cm thick. I like to use a mandolin to ensure even thickness, but you can also use a sharp knife.
3. Combine fries, oil, cinnamon and a large pinch of salt in a large bowl. Toss until evenly coated.
4. Spread fries over the lined tray and bake for 20 minutes or until golden and crisp, turning once or twice during the cooking time. Serve.

ZUCCHINI CHIPS

dairy-free / gluten-free /
grain-free / wheat-free

Zucchini are about 95 per cent water so I recommend
cutting them into thin discs so that they crisp up
more than when they're thicker. Zucchini are great
when spiralised, grated and tossed with olive oil and
lemon juice for a salad, or like this – in rounds as chips.

Makes 10

1 large zucchini
(about 200 g)
1 egg

¼ cup (30 g) ground
almonds
¼ cup (30 g) pistachio
kernels, finely chopped

Zucchini are packed with
nutritional goodness: vitamins
A and C, magnesium, folate,
potassium, copper and
phosphorus. They're also a
good source of dietary fibre.

The Queen of Sheba ordered
that pistachios be an
exclusively royal food. I wonder
if she knew how good they
are for fuelling the brain with
protein, fibre, magnesium,
phosphorus, vitamin B6 . . .

1. Preheat the oven to 200°C. Line a baking tray with
   baking paper.
2. Cut the zucchini into rounds, about 5 mm thick. I like to
   use a mandolin to ensure they are the same thickness
   and cook evenly. The thinner they are the crisper they
   will become.
3. Crack the egg into a shallow bowl and lightly whisk.
   Place the ground almonds and pistachios in two separate
   shallow bowls.
4. Dust each piece of zucchini in the almond meal, then coat
   in the egg, allowing any excess to drip off. Place into the
   pistachio and coat evenly on one side.
5. Spread zucchini nut side up over the lined tray and bake
   for 15 minutes or until golden and crisp. Allow to cool
   before eating.

SALT AND VINEGAR CHIPS (SORT OF!)

dairy-free / egg-free / gluten-free /
grain-free / nut-free / wheat-free

I use kipfler potatoes for this as they usually
come in near perfect chip shapes – long and thin!
Just remember to wash them well as their skin
sometimes holds on to dirt. These are also delicious
cold with a little dollop of tomato relish.

Makes about 16

4 kipfler potatoes
(about 400 g)
¼ cup (60 ml) white
vinegar
2 tablespoons olive oil

sea salt and ground
black pepper
2 sprigs of fresh rosemary
(optional)

1. Preheat the oven to 180°C. Line a baking tray with baking
   paper.
2. Wash potatoes well but don't worry about peeling them.
   Put them into a large saucepan. Cover with cold water
   and add the vinegar. Bring to the boil over a high heat,
   then reduce heat and simmer for 10–12 minutes or until
   almost tender. Drain.
3. Without burning your fingers, cut potatoes lengthwise
   so they look like big fat chips. Place on the prepared tray
   and drizzle with the olive oil. Season with salt and pepper.
   Sprigs of rosemary add a lovely flavour too.
4. Bake for 10–15 minutes or until golden and crisp, turning
   them a couple of times to ensure they cook evenly.
   Eat and enjoy!

Kipflers are also known as the
German Finger Potato and the
Austrian Crescent! The potato's
fibre, potassium, vitamin C and
B6 content, together with the
fact that it is low in cholesterol,
all help heart health.

It is a historical fact that
Hippocrates prescribed vinegar
and honey to treat cuts,
coughs and 17 other ailments.
Contemporary researchers
suggest that vinegar may play
a role in improving cholesterol,
not to mention being useful
for people who want to keep
their blood sugar levels low.

Put some gloves on
or use tongs!

Olive oil is extremely high
in oleic acid, which can help
to reduce blood pressure.

The most relevant benefits for
the study-stressed teenager are
rosemary's potential to boost
memory and improve mood!

CAULIFLOWER BLISS BOMBS

dairy-free / egg-free / gluten-free /
grain-free / nut-free / wheat-free

These bite-sized flavour bombs are not really a
chip, wedge or fry with their roundish shape, but they're
cooked like my other chips and are fantastic served as
an afternoon snack in a little container with a fork.
For those kids who don't love steamed cauliflower,
roasting it creates a different taste and texture entirely.
Serve golden from the oven or with spices sprinkled
over the top, which I call magic dust, because, well,
they bring some magic to the dish.

Makes about 20

1 head of cauliflower
   (about 1.5 kg)
1 tablespoon coconut oil
   (or olive oil)
sea salt and ground
   black pepper

1–2 tablespoons spice mix,
   such as Indian garam
   masala, Egyptian dukkha,
   Middle Eastern za'atar or
   Moroccan ras el hanout

1. Preheat the oven to 200°C. Line a large baking tray with
   baking paper.
2. Cut the cauliflower into bite-sized florets of equal size.
   Place in a bowl with oil and season with your choice of
   spices. Stir so cauliflower is evenly coated.
3. Transfer to the lined baking tray and roast for 25–30
   minutes or until golden and crispy.
4. Divide into little bowls or ramekins, sprinkle with salt and
   pepper and eat with a fork while still warm.

RECIPE LIST

CHOCOLATE MOUSSE

PERFECT PARFAIT

ROASTED VEG FRITTATA

BAKED BANANAS

COCONUT RICE

PORRIDGE THREE WAYS

BROWN RICE, COCONUT OIL AND HEMP SEEDS

TURMERIC LATTE

5

MIDNIGHT

MUNCHIES

ARE YOUR TEENAGERS BURNING THE MIDNIGHT OIL to get through their exams? Here are some midnight munchies to help them push through or wind down.

When it comes to eating late at night it's probably more important to think about what NOT to eat. Foods that are salty, spicy, sugary and fatty should be avoided because they can wreak havoc with digestion and sleep patterns. So, cross off takeaway cheesy pizza, creamy pasta, big serves of burgers and fries, and spicy curry dishes. Cross off commercially manufactured chocolate and chips, too. Red meat is hard to digest late at night and energy drinks are off the list, of course, because they are full of sugar and other stimulants which make it hard to nod off when study is done.

However, there are loads of things that students CAN eat. Simple food works best, and a light snack that is full of complex carbohydrates and a little protein is ideal.

Bananas are brilliant in the evening because they are full of magnesium, which can help aid relaxation. This can simply be a banana straight up or cut in half and smeared with almond butter. Even better are my Baked Bananas (see recipe page 106).

Other good midnight munchies ideas are half a mashed avocado or a hard-boiled egg on a piece of wholemeal toast, or some fresh fruit like an apple, grapes or strawberries (if in season) with a handful of nuts – a particularly good combo is a granny smith apple and 5 almonds. Corn on the cob is another super snack because it's so easy to prepare – just 2–3 minutes on HIGH in the microwave or boiled on the stove for 5–7 minutes.

Avoid big serves of anything – even the good stuff in the following pages should be snacked on in moderation. The body is naturally trying to wind down at night, not working hard at digestion.

If it's unavoidable to eat late owing to sport or social commitments, remember to allow time for digestion before your tired teen hits the sack, too – otherwise they could end up with a tummy ache if they lie down straight away after they've eaten. If they're really tired, you could suggest that they have a big glass of warm water or a relaxing Turmeric Latte (see recipe page 111) and just crash, instead of eating anything.

And one last note: while we've labelled these dishes 'midnight munchies', they work just as well at 9 p.m. or even 9 a.m.!

That's right, Flip – and in fact, I do not recommend that students study late at night as research shows we don't remember much when we are tired!

Here's a challenge: stand outside a typical school in a typical suburb of an Australian city at around 8.30 a.m. As students emerge from cars, buses and trams, an ocean of sleepy faces and hands holding lattes appears before us. It's narcolepsy central. Within half an hour, some of these young people will be completely zonked out, fast asleep with their heads on desks, while others will be so sleep-deprived that they are oblivious to the learning going on around them.

It's official: Australian teenagers – boys and girls – are one of the most sleep-deprived segments of the population. One of the world's leading authorities on teenage sleep, Brown University's Professor Mary Carskadon, is adamant that teenagers around the western world are unequivocally not getting enough sleep. Her research has found that on average, most adolescents are getting about 7.5 hours' sleep on school nights, though 25 per cent of them get 6.5 hours or fewer. However, Carskadon has found that in order for a young person to be optimally alert, they require 9.25 hours of sleep per night.

It is increasingly evident to educators and psychologists right across Australia that night after night, many boys and girls are treating sleep as an optional extra, and by doing so are building colossal sleep debts. If you attached an electroencephalograph (EEG) to those dozing students first thing in the morning, you'd see that 50 per cent of them would go directly into REM sleep – exhibiting the same brain waves as patients with narcolepsy. While these teenagers don't actually have narcolepsy, they're nevertheless living under conditions that actually make them appear as if they do.

Insufficient sleep not only impacts on teenagers' physical health, mood and cognitive ability but also dramatically reduces their capacity to perform and respond appropriately while sitting in a classroom, driving a car, playing sport or interacting with adult carers. From an academic point of view, the jury has well and truly given its verdict: sleep is the most important study tool going around. So, what to do about the issue? Well, schools must start teaching 'bed-ucation' because adolescents need to know how a lack of sleep impacts on their 100 billion brain cells and the trillion connections between them. Their adult carers need to step up to the parenting plate, make sleep a priority and set limits and boundaries around bedtime from an early age. And finally, perhaps we need to start reviewing school start times to create a system that meets the developmental needs of students instead of the adults who teach them. For my list of top study tips, see page 25.

CHOCOLATE MOUSSE

dairy-free / egg-free / gluten-free /
grain-free / nut-free / wheat-free

If your child is looking for a sugar fix late at night,
with this mousse they can satisfy their cravings in
a more nourishing way. Avocados are full of healthy
monounsaturated fats, high in fibre, and contain
20 vitamins and minerals. Choose avocados that are ripe
but not overly ripe and remove any bruises. This chocolate
mousse will last a couple of days in the fridge, so make a
big batch and have it at the ready. Allow enough time to
let it chill in the fridge for a few hours for the best flavour
and texture before eating. It's great topped with toasted
flaked coconut, blueberries and pomegranate seeds but
you can add any seasonal fruit you like.

Arrgghh they should
be asleep in bed!

Makes 4

2 firm ripe avocados,
  peeled, stone removed
½ cup (125 ml) canned
  coconut milk
¼ cup (25 g) cacao powder
2 tablespoons coconut oil,
  melted

1 teaspoon ground
  cinnamon
1–2 tablespoons coconut
  syrup, maple syrup or
  honey (optional)
shredded or flaked coconut
  and fresh berries, to serve

1. Put the avocados, coconut milk, cacao powder, coconut
   oil, cinnamon and coconut syrup (if using) into a food
   processor and process until completely smooth.
2. Divide mixture between 4 × 250 ml ramekins. Cover and
   place in the fridge for 2–3 hours (or overnight) to chill.
   Serve topped with coconut and berries.

Blueberries are preferable!

PERFECT PARFAIT

dairy-free (option) / egg-free /
gluten-free (option) / grain-free (option) /
nut-free (option) / wheat-free

Parfait is French for 'perfect', and this is one perfect breakfast-meets-dessert-meets-midnight-snack dish! You can assemble this snack in minutes and enjoy it straight away or make portions ahead of time. If you do make them ahead of time, the muesli will soften a little from the moisture of the berries and yoghurt – but that's not a bad thing depending on personal preference. For more crunch, use toasted muesli, but check the label to make sure it's not loaded with oil or sugar. If you don't have any toasted muesli, make your own. Place muesli on a lined baking tray, and dry-roast in a 200°C preheated oven for 10 minutes or until golden brown, stirring a couple of times to ensure the ingredients cook evenly and don't burn. Allow to cool before using. Opt for gluten-free muesli if necessary.

Makes 1

Every 100 g serving of rhubarb provides 45 per cent of the daily value in vitamin K, which promotes healthy bone growth and can reduce neuronal damage in the brain!

¼ cup (60 ml) canned coconut cream (or coconut yoghurt or Greek-style yoghurt)
¼ cup (25 g) natural muesli

¼ cup (about 40 g) fresh berries or stewed fruit (apple and rhubarb are delish)

1. Layer the ingredients in a tall, clear glass, starting with the coconut cream, followed by the muesli, then fruit.

TIP: This snack isn't going to fail if you don't layer in that order, nor if you don't have a tall clear glass! A small bowl with the ingredients side by side is great.

ROASTED VEG FRITTATA

gluten-free / grain-free /
nut-free / wheat-free

This dish is perfect to make with leftover roast veggies.
When I'm roasting veg, my rule of thumb is to always
make more than I need because I can use what's
left during the following days for this dish.
The quantities below make one serve, but simply double,
triple or quadruple the quantities to make more.

Makes 1

1 cup (about 150 g) roasted
  vegetables
  (such as onion, pumpkin,
  zucchini , carrot, potato)
1 tablespoon chopped
  pitted olives and/or
  sundried tomato strips
  (optional)

2 eggs
dash of milk
1–2 tablespoons grated
  parmesan cheese
sea salt and ground
  black pepper
tomato relish, to serve

1. Preheat the oven to 200°C.
2. Put the vegetables, olives and sundried tomato (if using)
   in a 1½ cup/375 ml capacity ramekin. Whisk the eggs,
   milk and parmesan cheese together in a small bowl.
   Pour over the veggies and season with salt and pepper.
3. Bake for 20 minutes or until golden, set and puffed.
   Serve with a dollop of relish .

Always use zucchini (which my mum called courgette) when doing roasted veggies. Just one medium-sized zucchini is packed with 50 per cent of our daily vitamin C needs, a vitamin which supports the crucial lining of the blood cells, lowers blood pressure and protects against inflammation.

Parmesan is an excellent source of calcium.

I am a big fan of sundried tomatoes. They are a good source of dietary fibre, iron, magnesium, phosphorus, potassium, vitamins C and K . . . basically, brain rapture!

If I had a restaurant, I'd call it 'A Dollop of Relish'!

BAKED BANANAS

dairy-free / egg-free / gluten-free /
grain-free / nut-free / wheat-free

This dish is one of my favourite comfort foods and for good reason – bananas contain tryptophan and vitamin B6 which converts to serotonin, the good mood hormone.

Excuse me, who is the psychologist here?!

Serves 2

2 bananas
1 cup (250 ml) fresh orange
   juice (about 2 oranges)
¼ cup (40 g) sultanas (or
   currants or other dried
   fruit)

1 tablespoon shredded
   coconut
ground cinnamon, to
   sprinkle

1. Preheat the oven to 180°C.

One of the most ancient fruits going around – recent archaeological evidence in Papua New Guinea suggests that banana cultivation there goes back to at least 5000 BC, and possibly to 8000 BC!

2. Peel the bananas and place side by side in a baking dish which fits them comfortably but is not too roomy. Pour in the orange juice, then add the sultanas and coconut and sprinkle with cinnamon.

3. Cover the dish with foil and bake for 30 minutes or until the bananas have softened. You can cook this dish without the foil if you remember to baste the bananas with the orange juice regularly, so the bananas don't dry out. This is best served warm but can be eaten cold.

COCONUT RICE

dairy-free / egg-free / gluten-free / nut-free / wheat-free / freezable

Rice pudding is traditionally made with sugar and cream, so this is a healthier alternative . It's easy to make and requires little effort – it's just a matter of setting the timer. This recipe makes more rice than needed for one snack serving so use the amount required, then put the rest in a couple of containers and place in the fridge or freezer for another time.

Adding coconut to rice boosts its benefits for the body: coconut nourishes good bacteria in the large intestine to help keep the gut healthy,[22] but a word of warning: the good bacteria can produce some flatulence!

Serves 4

2 cups (400 g) medium grain white rice
2 cups (500 ml) water
1 cup (250 ml) canned coconut milk or cream
1 teaspoon ground cinnamon or ginger

grated palm sugar or raw brown sugar, to serve
sliced fresh mango or banana, to serve
toasted coconut flakes, to serve

Palm sugar is an unrefined sugar. It is known to contain vitamins and minerals, and is therefore a better choice than white sugar.

1. Put the rice, water, coconut milk or cream and your chosen spice into a large saucepan and bring to the boil over high heat. Reduce heat to low and hold at a gentle simmer, covered, for 12 minutes. Do not lift the lid, do not stir!

2. Remove from heat and allow rice to stand, covered, for 10 minutes. (Again, don't lift the lid!)

3. Top with a small amount of grated palm or raw brown sugar. Serve with fresh mango, sliced banana or toasted coconut flakes – or all three.

Do not pass Go!
Do not collect $200!

Bossy!

PORRIDGE THREE WAYS

dairy-free / nut-free / wheat-free

The high fibre content in porridge may boost digestion, lower high blood cholesterol and help prevent heart disease. Porridge consists of whole grains, which have both soluble and insoluble fibre. The insoluble fibre stimulates movement of waste and helps relieve constipation, while soluble fibre helps reduce glucose levels and low-density lipoprotein blood cholesterol.

Who said porridge is *just* for breakfast? It makes the best midnight snack because it's warming and nourishing. Really, there are no limitations when it comes to how you serve it. Sure, you can do as celebrity chef Heston Blumenthal does and serve your porridge with snails and bacon, but here are a few simpler ideas. Because these are savoury dishes, I recommend cooking the rolled oats with water or a mild vegetable stock rather than milk. As Goldilocks will attest, everyone likes their porridge a bit different! Some have it thick enough to stand a spoon upright in it, while others prefer something smoother. I've included three different cooking options here depending on your preference and the time available. One serve is ⅓ cup (30 g) of rolled oats, but this can be adjusted according to need and taste. Simply multiply the measurements by the number of mouths you need to feed.

Quick sticks porridge

1. Put ⅓ cup (30 g) rolled (traditional) oats in a small bowl.
2. Add ⅓ cup (80 ml) boiling water.
3. Cover with plastic film or a small plate and set aside for 5–10 minutes, or until the oats have absorbed all the water.

Thick and creamy porridge

1. Place ⅓ cup (30 g) rolled (traditional) oats and ⅔ cup (160 ml) boiling water in a saucepan.
2. Leave to stand for 10 minutes.
3. Cook over medium heat, stirring, for 2 minutes or until thick and creamy.

Microwave porridge

1. Add ½ cup (45 g) rolled (traditional) oats and 1 cup (250 ml) water or vegetable stock to a microwave-safe container.

2. Cover the container loosely with the lid to let steam escape. Microwave on medium (50 per cent) for 3 minutes.

3. Leave to stand for 2–3 minutes or until the liquid is absorbed and the porridge is thick. Stir and transfer to a warmed bowl.

Topping ideas

- A hard-boiled egg and baby rocket leaves (arugula)
- A simple seasoning of sea salt and cracked black pepper
- Sweet Potato Fries (see recipe page 94)
- Some smashed avocado, a few chopped cherry tomatoes and a small handful of dry-roasted almonds
- Some chopped sundried tomatoes, a dollop of pesto and a few shavings of parmesan cheese
- Some protein-rich cooked lentils, blanched spinach and a sprinkling of nutritional yeast, stirred through

Studies suggest that increasing consumption of plant foods like rocket (arugula) reduces the risks of obesity, diabetes and heart disease, as well as promoting a healthy complexion, boosting energy and lowering overall weight.

BROWN RICE, COCONUT OIL AND HEMP SEEDS

dairy-free / egg-free / gluten-free /
nut-free / wheat-free / freezable

Brown rice is a complex carbohydrate that can help relax the body, while coconut oil is an anti-inflammatory and hemp seeds are packed full of omega-3 and -6 to help brain cells. I always have cooked brown rice at the ready. This dish is quick to make and easy to digest, which makes it great at night but also a good option for breakfast, especially for tummies unsettled by nerves. I love the subtle flavour of these three fabulous ingredients.

Serves 1

½ cup (85 g) cooked brown rice (room temperature or just warmed)

1 tablespoon coconut oil, melted
1–2 teaspoons hemp seeds

The *seeds* of the hemp plant are definitely the part that promotes health – and they won't make anyone high or fail a drug test! In fact, they're a great source of plant-based protein and are packed full of great stuff like magnesium, calcium, iron and zinc.

1. Put all the ingredients into a small bowl and stir to combine. Eat and enjoy.
2. A sprinkling of freshly chopped parsley and a little salt and pepper are also nice additions.

TIP: Cooked brown rice can be stored in the fridge for several days, and frozen for up to a month. If storing, cool rice as quickly as possible (ideally within 1 hour) after cooking and store in a refrigerator below 5°C.

TURMERIC LATTE

dairy-free (option) / egg-free
gluten-free / grain-free / nut-free / wheat-free

Turmeric has fabulous calming qualities – perfect when it's time to hit the sack after studying for a few hours .

Makes 1

1 teaspoon ground turmeric
¼ teaspoon ground
   cinnamon, plus extra to
   sprinkle
small pinch of ground
   black pepper

1 teaspoon maple syrup
   (or honey)
1 cup (250 ml) milk of your
   chioce (dairy, rice, soy,
   oat, almond)

Luckily I am here to educate you, Flip: we do not recommend that students study for hours at a time! We recommend breaking up studying into a series of 20-minute chunks – so a turmeric latte would be perfect for a break in between sessions.

1. Combine the spices and honey with 1 tablespoon hot water in a heat-proof cup or mug and stir to make a paste.
2. Warm the milk in a small saucepan over medium heat to your desired temperature. Pour the milk over the spice paste and stir until well combined.
3. Serve with an additional sprinkling of cinnamon.

RECIPE LIST

'AVE AN AVO

BERRY GOOD IDEA

THE SIX CS

MAKE IT A DATE

APPLE SANDWICH

CELERY BOATS

SPINACH SOUP

CHINESE PUDDING

BLANCHED GREENS

SUPER-SPEEDY EGG

BANANA BITES

D.I.Y. YOGHURT POT

6

FAST
FOOD

WE'RE ALL FAMILIAR WITH THOSE TIMES when our kids are hangry and have to eat NOW.

'Hangry' is a modern term, a combination of 'hungry' and 'angry' used to describe being irritable or angry due to hunger.

When we are hangry our blood sugar level has dropped, making it hard to think clearly, and that's when bad food choices are much more likely to be made. The temptation is to immediately reach for snacks or drinks high in simple sugars, which certainly do give us an energy spike and temporarily ease those feelings. But with simple sugars, what goes up must come down.

A snack full of simple sugars does not sustain or satisfy us for any useful length of time, and while our energy might increase immediately after eating the snack (that 'hyper' feeling we get), our energy (and mood) will take a dive. Hunger will strike again, so we pick ourselves up with something sugary again, and round and round the not-so-merry-go-round we go.

Hunger is often dehydration in disguise, so start your child off with a big glass of water. (For more information on this, see Hydration, page 16.) When they've drunk the water, direct them to the fruit bowl to grab some grapes or pick up a pear. These are the original and best fast foods!

If that still doesn't do the trick, then try one of the ideas in this chapter. The following snacks are quick and easy to prepare but the key to smart snacks is being organised, so ensure the ingredients are always in stock at home. Likewise, if you know that the kids – or you – can't resist chocolate or biscuits when hangry (which can easily turn into a block of chocolate and an entire packet of biscuits), simply don't buy them. You can't eat what's not in the cupboard.

Another good tool for smart snacking at times of hanger is to have an 'Eat This' list stuck on the fridge. You can either photocopy the recipe list from this chapter or make your own, according to what you've got at home each week.

When you need to get something in front of your child immediately, choose snacks that are high in good fats, like avocado, as this satisfies hunger quickly because it registers satiety with the brain. Nuts and seeds are also high in essential fatty acids, though they're easy to overeat, especially when really hungry. Another good choice is food that's high in fibre, like fruit and veggies. And finally, foods high in complex carbohydrates, like basmati or brown rice, make fantastic snacks to ward off low energy levels and bad moods.

Chewing food properly is essential for proper digestion and also helps the brain to register that our tummy has food on the way and no longer needs to rumble. While my gran was fond of saying, '100 chews for every mouthful, my dear,' I suggest chewing slowly with the eyes closed. It's amazing what the simple act of closing our eyes does to slow down our eating and heart rate. Taking away our sense of sight means our other senses are heightened. This enhances flavour perception, brings mindfulness to the moment and allows the whole body to register that food is here!

'AVE AN AVO

dairy-free / egg-free / gluten-free /
grain-free / nut-free / wheat-free

Have an avocado . Cut it in half, drizzle with a squeeze of lemon juice and season with salt and pepper. The fat in the avocado encourages the feeling of satisfaction and helps prevent overeating – which can happen easily at times of severe and mindless hunger!

BERRY GOOD IDEA

dairy-free / egg-free / gluten-free /
grain-free / nut-free / wheat-free

A punnet of berries – strawberries , blueberries, blackberries or raspberries – is convenient, delicious and nutritious. Summer is the best season to buy and eat berries as they taste best then. Frozen berries are great for cooking and making smoothies but they never taste as good as the fresh ones when eaten raw. Buying in season, which I strongly recommend whenever possible, means they're also a cheap smart snack.

THE SIX CS

dairy-free / egg-free / gluten-free /
grain-free / nut-free / wheat-free

Celery, cucumber , carrots, cherry tomatoes,
snow and sugar snap peas.

Cucumber is good for contributing to our daily vitamin C intake.

Place a colourful medley of cherry tomatoes in their own bowl on the bench. Chop then place all the other veggies in the fridge in clear containers at the front of the shelves at eye level so they are the first things your child sees when they open the fridge. Stick some notes like 'Eat me first', 'Start here' and 'Pick me! Pick me!' on the containers. This helps the decision-making process when kids are starving and can't think clearly .

Such clever psychology!

Snow and sugar snap peas start with 's' but sound like 'c' so they make the list; besides, they're also brilliant as they've got a great crunch and a sweetness to them.

MAKE IT A DATE

dairy-free / egg-free / gluten-free /
grain-free / wheat-free

Remove the pip from a medjool date and replace it with a walnut then sprinkle with cinnamon. This tastes so good and will satisfy sweet tooths in an instant. If you squint, it even looks like a Tim Tam – but it's full of fibre and rich in vitamins and minerals.

APPLE SANDWICH

dairy-free / egg-free / gluten-free /
grain-free / wheat-free

Did you know that green apples are rich in a bioflavonoid called quercetin, a natural antihistamine and anti-inflammatory? To boot, they have natural antiviral and anti-fungal properties – so perhaps that old cliché 'an apple a day' holds some truth . . .

Using a corer, remove the core of an apple , then slice it into 1–2 cm-thick rounds. Spread one slice with nut butter, add a few cacao nibs and then put another slice on top. Repeat with the other slices. The combination of fat and protein from the nuts, with the fibre and carbohydrate from the apple, will help curb hunger pangs. Lots of different nut butters – almond, cashew, macadamia and delicious combinations – are now readily available in supermarkets. Just remember to check the label to make sure the jar doesn't contain any extras like oils, sugar or other nasties.

TIP: chopped apple
It might seem like a silly idea, but when I chop an apple and eat it in pieces I eat more slowly, which is better for digestion. Sometimes I eat a whole apple quickly because I don't put it down. So, if you don't have a corer or any nut butter in the cupboard, cut up the kids' apples to create a more mindful snack.

CELERY BOATS

egg-free / gluten-free / grain-free / nut-free /
wheat-free

Celery is a brilliant source of potassium and a good source of manganese, vitamin K, beta-carotene, folate and dietary fibre. And the leaves are the most nutritious part, so you can save them and finely chop them to add to a salad or a pesto.

Fill celery sticks with ricotta or cottage cheese. Gently press in a few sultanas and sprinkle with cinnamon. Easy to make and even easier to eat! This was one of my favourite childhood snacks and I still love it.

SPINACH SOUP

egg-free / gluten-free / grain-free /
nut-free / wheat-free

Add several big handfuls of baby spinach leaves to a pan
of boiling water. Turn off heat and blanch for 1 minute.

Save ½ cup (125 ml) water in case you want to thin the soup.
Drain the rest and blend in a food processor. Season with
salt and pepper, add a dollop of ricotta for a creamier blend
or a splash of lemon juice, and it's ready to eat or drink!
The vitamin C in the lemon juice can help the absorption
of the iron in the spinach, while adding some fat in
the form of ricotta can assist the absorption of
some vitamins and minerals.

Genius, Flip! Especially
because cooking spinach
actually ratchets up some
of its nutritional benefits,
such as the absorption of
the vitamins A and E, zinc,
calcium and iron it contains.

CHINESE PUDDING

egg-free / gluten-free (option) / nut-free / wheat-free

I don't know the true origin of this recipe but my
husband's grandmother was Chinese and she used to
give this to him. Mix together 1 cup (170 g) cooked rice,
1–2 teaspoons soy sauce or tamari (for a gluten-free
version), 1–2 teaspoons butter and a sprinkling of
toasted sesame seeds. This is the sublime combination
of sweet, salty and umami flavours.

This snack combines old
and new: sesame seeds have
been cultivated for more than
3500 years but umami, the
pleasant savoury 'fifth taste'
after salt, sweet, sour and bitter,
was only coined as a scientific
term in the twentieth century.

BLANCHED GREENS

dairy-free / egg-free / gluten-free /
grain-free / nut-free / wheat-free

Always have a stash of seasonal greens such as asparagus, broccolini, green beans and snow or sugar snap peas at the ready to blanch in boiling water for 1–2 minutes. Once cooked, drizzle them with a little oil (sesame, olive, coconut or macadamia) and sprinkle with sesame seeds for a flavour burst that kids will enjoy.

Don't underestimate the value of consuming some fat such as the oil recommended alongside the buffet of green veg in order to supercharge your child's nutrient absorption. Fat helps us to absorb vitamins A, D, E and K.

SUPER-SPEEDY EGG

dairy-free (option) / gluten-free / grain-free /
nut-free / wheat-free

For a quick protein hit to satisfy that hungry child or teen, this is an eggsellent idea. Keep it simple and break an egg into a microwave-safe ramekin or mug. Using a skewer or fork, pierce the egg yolk a few times to prevent it from exploding. Cover the container with plastic film.

For soft-centred eggs, microwave on HIGH (100 per cent) for 30 seconds. For hard-centred eggs, microwave on HIGH (100 per cent) for 40 seconds. Stand for 30 seconds then remove the plastic film. Season with salt and pepper and add chopped fresh herbs like parsley or chives.

For something more substantial, whisk together an egg with a splash of milk, add 1 tablespoon grated cheese, chopped tomato, capsicum and mushrooms. Season with salt and pepper. Transfer to a microwave safe ramekin or mug. Cover with plastic film. Microwave on HIGH (100 per cent) for 30 seconds.

Eggs contain the micronutrient choline, a building block of an important neurotransmitter called acetylcholine which is crucial for learning, memory and neuroplasticity. The science is clear that up to three whole eggs a day is safe for healthy people who are trying to stay so, and they also have the benefit of elevating HDL, the 'good' cholesterol.

BANANA BITES

dairy-free (option) / egg-free / gluten-free /
grain-free / wheat-free / nut-free (option)

Peel a banana then chop it into bite-sized rounds.
Top with a dollop of macadamia nut butter or ricotta,
add a few coconut flakes and dust with cinnamon.
Again, try to encourage your child to slow down the eating
process by closing their eyes and focusing on what they're
chewing, which they often find fun. Get them to describe
the taste and texture – but not with their mouth full!

D.I.Y. YOGHURT POT

egg-free / gluten-free / grain-free /
nut-free (option) / wheat-free

Yoghurt is a good source of protein and fat. Yoghurt is
a fat source by its very nature, so to produce a no-fat or
low-fat yoghurt means replacing the naturally occurring
fats with a high amount of sugar or other fillers, which is
why I always recommend opting for full-fat plain dairy
products. To add flavour to plain yoghurt, stir through
whole or puréed berries, stewed or grated apple, chopped
or mashed banana, a few nuts and seeds, or a sprinkling
of cinnamon and nutmeg topped with some freshly
chopped mint. Now *that's* deluxe.

RECIPE LIST

WATERMELON AND RASPBERRY ICY POLES

MANGO AND COCONUT ICE-CREAMS

FRUITCICLES

AVOCADO ICE-CREAMS

CARAMEL AND CHOC CHIP ICE-CREAMS

BANANARAMA ICE-CREAMS

VEGGIE POLES

UP BEET

HAPPY WATER

ICED TEA

7

COOL THINGS FOR HOT HEADS

STUDYING CAN BE FRUSTRATING, HARD WORK, especially during a hot summer, so encourage your kids to schedule regular breaks and use the ten ideas in this chapter to cool hot heads with some refreshing icy poles, healthy ice-creams and thirst-quenching drinks.

While store-bought ice-creams are enticing, especially in their colourfully alluring packaging, you might like to reconsider them as an afternoon treat.

Ice-cream was traditionally made with just cream, milk and eggs, but today many commercially produced ice-creams contain reconstituted milk, glucose syrup, wheat, vegetable oil, vegetable gum, emulsifiers, maltodextrin and sugar as well as flavour and colouring. Meanwhile, sugar and artificial colours and flavourings have snuck into some store-bought icy poles and gelato.

Instead, why not make your own icy poles and ice-creams? None of my recipes require an ice-cream maker, and imagination is the only limit when it comes to the possible flavour combinations. They are so simple and easy to make that the kids can do it themselves. And most importantly, you will know exactly what they are made of. A delicious, nutritious snack is just a lick away!

There are numerous icy pole moulds available, ranging in price (from just a few dollars to a small fortune) and size (with sets of four to sixteen). You can buy plastic or stainless steel grids, but I love the individual silicone icy

Correct, Flip, go to the top of the class! Research shows that no one should study for longer than 20 minutes in a row without taking a break.

pole moulds because they can fit into the freezer at all different angles and wherever there is space.

Each different style of icy pole mould holds a different volume, so measure their capacity and then adjust the following recipes. If you do have any mixture left over, either drink it on the spot (as of course all icy pole mixtures are drinkable) or transfer it to an ice-block mould to be enjoyed at another time. In fact, if you don't have an icy pole mould, don't worry. Simply pour the mixture into an ice-block mould and create icy pole 'cubes' or minis which the kids can pop into their mouths to suck and savour.

An icy pole never fails to hit the spot on a summer's day, and because I never know when a horde of hot and sweaty kids are going to walk through the door, I always make them ahead of time so the freezer has a ready supply. Likewise, it's handy to have some available for older students' study breaks. Grabbing a homemade icy pole from the freezer is an enjoyable experience but it also has an end point, at which time the resident scholar can head back to their desk.

Encourage your kids to maximise their enjoyment of the icy pole by being mindful . This simply means paying full attention to the experience – both internally and externally – focusing on the colours, smells, textures, flavours, temperatures and even the sounds of the icy pole or drink. An icy pole is even better when eaten in the fresh air, with your sock-free feet feeling some cool grass or water.

They could also try my favourite stress reliever smart phone app, Smiling Mind, which promotes mindfulness meditation.

WATERMELON AND RASPBERRY ICY POLES

dairy-free / egg-free / gluten-free / grain-free /
nut-free / wheat-free / freezable

Mine was the Golden Gaytime!

One of my favourite childhood ice-creams was the classic Raspberry Split. You can make a modern-day version of that with layers of crushed raspberries and thick plain Greek yoghurt, but here is a super simple version made with watermelon which is 99 per cent water and therefore very refreshing.

Makes 6–8

2 cups (280 g) chopped seedless watermelon

1 cup (125 g) fresh or frozen raspberries

Raspberries come from the same botanical family as the rose and the blackberry. They have more vitamin C than the humble orange and are super high in fibre and folic acid.

1. Put the watermelon and raspberries into a blender or food processor and blend until smooth.
2. Pour mixture into icy pole moulds (you will need 6–8 moulds depending upon size). Place lids on the moulds and freeze for 8 hours or overnight. Serve.

MANGO AND COCONUT ICE-CREAMS

dairy-free / egg-free / gluten-free / grain-free /
nut-free / wheat-free / freezable

These ice-creams are holidays on a stick because they have a lovely tropical flavour! I use canned Asian-style coconut milk because it gives them a creamy taste and smooth texture. You can use coconut milk in a carton but it has a significantly thinner consistency and contains only about 10 per cent coconut milk, making it less flavoursome.

Makes 6–8

2 cups (250 g) chopped fresh or frozen mango
1 cup (250 ml) canned coconut milk
1 teaspoon ground cinnamon
2 tablespoons toasted coconut flakes

1 cup of mango contains absolutely no fat, cholesterol or sodium.

1. Put the mango, coconut milk and cinnamon into a blender. Blend until smooth. Stir in the coconut flakes.
2. Pour mixture into icy pole moulds (you will need 6–8 moulds depending upon size). Place lids on the moulds and freeze for 8 hours or overnight. Serve.

TIP: If you don't have mangoes at hand, banana, pineapple or cherries are also delicious alternatives.

FRUITCICLES

dairy-free / egg-free / gluten-free / grain-free /
nut-free / wheat-free / freezable

Grand Canyon, move over!

These look visually spectacular if you add lots of different colours and shapes. Most fruits work well so you can't go wrong: just choose the flavours you and the kids love. Fruitcicles are also a simple way to increase the amount of fruit eaten in a day.

Makes 6–8

2–3 cups (500–750 ml)
   coconut water
blueberries and
   raspberries, fresh
   or frozen
kiwi fruit , peeled
   and thinly sliced
strawberries, sliced thinly

mango, peeled and thinly
   sliced
starfruit, thinly sliced
grapes, left whole or
   cut into halves
banana, chopped into
   rounds

Also known as the Chinese gooseberry, it contains more vitamin C weight for weight than an orange! Kiwis are also high in vitamins A, B, E and K.

1. Half fill your icy pole moulds with coconut water.
2. Add your favourite fruit to each mould. You can add as much or as little fruit as you like.
3. Top up with coconut water so the moulds are almost full.
4. Freeze for 8 hours or overnight.

D.I.Y. Yoghurt Pot (page 121)

Fruitcicles (page 128) and Avocado Ice-Creams (page 129)

Happy Water (page 134) and Iced Tea (page 135)

Red Pesto (page 142), Gremolata (page 141) and Avocado and . . . (page 140)

Traffic Light Wrap (page 143)

Fruit Sticks (page 156)

Roasted Chickpeas (page 158), Salt and Pepper Coconut Chips (page 163) and Tamari Nuts (page 160)

Venus Bars (page 176)

Bountee Bites (page 174) and Cheery Ripes (page 172)

Brownie (page 180)

AVOCADO ICE-CREAMS (A.K.A. ICE-VOCADOS)

dairy-free / egg-free / gluten-free / grain-free /
nut-free / wheat-free / freezable

We love avos in everything, so why not ice-cream?! In fact,
avocados are rich and smooth so once blended are rather
like my mum's traditional ice-cream made with full fat
milk, double cream and egg yolks. And if you want
to make a chocolate version of this Ice-vocado, simply
add some cacao powder. Raw unprocessed cacao
(not cocoa powder) tastes like a decadent addition
but it's packed full of good stuff, like antioxidants,
iron, calcium and magnesium.

Makes 6–8

1 large ripe avocado ,
  peeled, stone removed
1 cup (250 ml) canned
  coconut milk
1 tablespoon maple syrup
  or honey

1 teaspoon ground
  cinnamon (optional)
1 tablespoon cacao powder
  (optional)

Listen up, mums and dads, this
one's for you: the oil in avocado
is reported to possess potent
anti-ageing properties that
protect against free radicals![23]

The antioxidant levels in
60 ml of maple syrup are
similar to a banana or a serve
of broccoli – amazing.

1. Put all the ingredients into a food processor and process
   until well combined and smooth. Taste and adjust with
   extra maple syrup or honey, cinnamon and cacao powder
   (if using) to suit.
2. Pour mixture into icy pole moulds (you will need
   6–8 moulds depending upon size). Place lids on the
   moulds and freeze for 4 hours or until firm. Serve.

CARAMEL AND CHOC CHIP ICE-CREAMS

dairy-free / egg-free / gluten-free / grain-free / nut-free / wheat-free / freezable

First found in Peru and cultivated since AD 200, lucuma is sky-high in carotene, iron, vitamin B3 and fibre, and its carotene content is great for aiding healthy eyesight.

This is a simple ice-cream with a sweet vanilla caramel flavour created by the lucuma powder, while the cacao nibs play the role of the choc chips. Lucuma powder can be found in most health food stores and it's worth the trip to find because it makes this ice-cream so delicious and unique. While cacao nibs and choc chips have the same origins, they are processed very differently and the two resulting products aren't that similar at all. Cacao nibs are the much healthier option. The best bit about this ice-cream is that it's ready to eat about an hour after making it. Either pop it in the fridge for a mousse-like texture or in the freezer for something a bit firmer.

Makes 2–4

1 cup (250 ml) canned coconut cream
½ cup (75 g) lucuma powder (see Tip)

1 tablespoon cacao nibs

1. Put the coconut cream and lucuma into a blender and blend until well combined. Stir through the cacao nibs.
2. Pour the mixture into individual ramekins or icy pole moulds (you will need 2–4 moulds depending upon size).
3. Cover and freeze for 1 hour or until firm.

TIP: Lucuma powder can be substituted with 1 tablespoon of vanilla extract for a vanilla choc chip ice-cream.

BANANARAMA ICE-CREAMS

dairy-free / egg-free / gluten-free /
grain-free / wheat-free / freezable

Barney Banana icy poles were one of my favourite childhood ice-creams, and are the inspiration behind this recipe. These are lovely and sweet – just like Michael Carr-Gregg!

Aw shucks!

Makes 4–6

½ cup (75 g) raw cashews
3 ripe bananas (the riper the better because the sweeter the taste)

1 teaspoon ground cinnamon
1 tablespoon vanilla extract

1. Put the cashews in a glass or ceramic bowl. Cover with cold water. Cover with plastic film and set aside in a cool place overnight to soak. Drain.
2. Put the bananas, cinnamon, vanilla and cashews in a food processor and process until smooth.
3. Pour the mixture into icy pole moulds (you will need 4–6 moulds depending upon size). Place lids on the moulds and freeze for 1 hour or until firm. Serve.

VEGGIE POLES

dairy-free / egg-free / gluten-free / grain-free /
nut-free / wheat-free / freezable

Yes, an icy pole made from veggies! Don't baulk –
it's delicious. Give it a go, I dare you! And if your child
doesn't like this combination of veg, try swapping
them for one that they do. Heat, stress and anxiety
can all have an impact on appetite so this is a fun and
gentle way to get some veg in. These veggie poles
can also be served on the side of a main meal –
a friend of mine did just that and her kids' eyes lit up
when they saw an icy pole on their dinner plate!

Makes 4–6

Cucumbers contain an anti-inflammatory brain-friendly substance called fisetin, plus the vitamin alphabet of B1, B2, B3, B5, B6, C and K. Not to mention folate, calcium, iron, magnesium, phosphorus, potassium and zinc . . . who needs a multivitamin!

1–2 Lebanese cucumbers,
   peeled and deseeded
400 g canned tomatoes
   (diced or whole)

2–3 basil leaves
1 tablespoon coconut oil
sea salt and ground black
   pepper

1. Put the cucumbers, tomatoes, basil and coconut oil
   into a blender and blend until smooth. Season to taste
   with a little salt and pepper.
2. Pour the mixture into icy pole moulds (you will need
   4–6 moulds depending upon size). Place lids on the
   moulds and freeze for 4 hours or overnight. Serve.

UP BEET

dairy-free / egg-free / gluten-free / grain-free /
nut-free / wheat-free / freezable

With its bright red colour, this icy pole looks fantastic!
I challenge your hot-headed son or daughter not to feel
good after eating this icy pole with all the immunity-
boosting vitamins and minerals contained in it. In fact,
more than once when I've prepared the ingredients to
make a batch, I've ended up pouring the mixture into
a tall clear glass and drinking it myself!

Makes 4–6

1 beetroot
1 large carrot
1 green apple, cored

½ cup (60 g) fresh
raspberries

1. Pass the beetroot, carrot and apple through a juicer.
2. Crush the raspberries with a fork and add to the vegetable
   mixture. Stir until well combined.
3. Pour the mixture into icy pole moulds (you will need
   4–6 moulds depending upon size). Place lids on the
   moulds and freeze for 8 hours or overnight. Serve.

Beetroot are high in nitrates which, when consumed, convert into nitric oxide, which reduces blood pressure and increases blood flow to the brain. In 1975, during the Apollo–Soyuz Test Project, cosmonauts from the USSR's Soyuz 19 welcomed the Apollo 18 astronauts by preparing a banquet of beetroot soup – in zero gravity. Neat trick!

HAPPY WATER

Make this at the start of each day and either keep it in a jug on the desk or in a bottle with a lid to carry and drink throughout the day. Just looking at colours can create positive feelings, but it will also keep hard-working students hydrated and healthy. The flavours will infuse over the course of the day and create a tastier drink. More water can be added to the jug or bottle as needed. The ingredients should last a couple of days so simply add more water and lemon juice on the next day – but I love to eat the blueberries, cucumber, mint leaves, ginger and turmeric as a refreshing snack at the end of each day.

Makes 2 litres

½ cup (75 g) blueberries (use frozen if you don't have fresh berries)
1 mini cucumber, sliced lengthways
small knob fresh ginger, peeled and grated
small knob fresh turmeric, peeld and grated
small handful (¼ cup) mint leaves
zest and juice of 1 lemon

Flip, did you know that the scent of mint has been found to excite the hippocampus in the brain, which controls mental clarity and memory? Recent research from Wheeling Jesuit University revealed that just the smell or flavor of peppermint has amazing effects on reasoning, problem solving, concept formation, judgement, attention span and even memory.[24] Plus it's a natural breath-freshener!

1. Put all the ingredients into a 2-litre container or jug. Top with enough cold water to fill. Drink throughout the day, adding more water as needed.
2. Once the water is finished, place blueberries and other ingredients in the fridge, covered, for the next day's brew or eat and start again.

ICED TEA

dairy-free / egg-free / gluten-free / grain-free /
nut-free / wheat-free / freezable

With so many different teas available these days, there's something to suit everyone and there's no risk of flavour fatigue. There's green, black or white; intense or mild flavours; herbal; floral, fruity or zesty teas. You can even make your own blend by combining different tea bags or tea leaves. I make a big jug of iced tea at the start of a hot day and keep it in the fridge so that whoever is at home can always pour themselves a glass. Remember that green, black and white teas do contain various levels of naturally occurring caffeine which isn't recommended for young students, especially primary school-aged kids.

Tea contains polyphenols, antioxidants that repair cells. An amino acid called L-theanine has been found in green tea, which traverses the blood–brain barrier and can increase the levels of neurotransmitters and alpha wave activity in the brain – how smart is that?

Makes 1.25 litres

1–2 teabags of your choice
1 cup (250 ml) boiling water

1 litre cold water

1. Put the teabags in a mug and top with the boiling water. Allow to steep for 3–5 minutes. The longer you leave the teabags in the water, the more intense the flavour. This is a matter of experimentation as each tea bag is different – as are we!
2. Remove tea bags and transfer the tea to a large jug. Fill with cold water.
3. Keep chilled in the fridge during the day.

RECIPE LIST

AVOCADO AND . . .

SAY CHEESE . . . AND VEGEMITE!

EGGSELLENT

GREMOLATA

ABC NUTTER

RED PESTO

ROASTED VEG

TRAFFIC LIGHT WRAP

QUESADILLA

HAPPY HUMMUS

SMASHED BANANA

FRUIT SANDWICH

8

SUPER SANGAS

SANDWICHES FILL MANY A SCHOOL LUNCHBOX but they are also perfect for afternoon tea because apart from being delicious, they can include all food groups. Wholegrain or rye bread brings complex carbohydrates to the table (pun intended!), veggies are full of filling fibre, while good fats come from things like avocado and plant-based proteins from nut butters. Sandwiches can be colourful and complex or plain and simple. Depending on the bread and filling you choose, they can be crunchy and chunky or sweet and smooth. They are really so versatile and, frankly, who doesn't love a sanga? All in all they're a substantial, satisfying snack.

While forms of the sandwich have appeared throughout history, it was the Earl of Sandwich who became the naming sponsor, so to speak. The story goes that the English aristocrat John Montagu, 4th Earl of Sandwich, liked to eat food that could be held in one hand so he could keep playing cards at the same time. He ordered his servant to place some cooked meat between two pieces of bread so his hands and cards didn't get greasy. It wasn't long before his mates at the card table started to order 'the same as Sandwich', and so the sandwich was born. What would the Earl of Sandwich think now, knowing that his right royal idea, created during the 1700s, is still eaten daily by common folk and loved around the world?

The bread used to make sandwiches is very important and something I am passionate about. Making bread is one of the oldest traditions but it was also one of the first foods to be mass produced because of technological advancements and the rise of commercial machinery. Soon, flour was being ground into a fine grain, bleached and turned into a cheap sliced product that was highly processed and nutritionally devoid. Now, thanks to the Slow Food movement, the rise of farmers' markets and the return of many talented artisan bakers, we've come full circle and are once again seeing a wonderful range of breads with different tastes and textures and full of nutrients.

Choosing different kinds of bread – whether it's wholegrain, sourdough, noir, rye, pumpernickel or even pumpkin – means kids can get access to a variety of grains, each with a slightly different nutritional profile. And for those with food intolerances, there are now some delicious gluten-free, FODMAP-friendly, yeast-free and even grain free bread options, which is fantastic.

What about Ezekiel bread? It's made from organic, sprouted whole grains and free of sugar and additives.

As for the filling? Well, a recent study by Victoria University revealed that people who eat Vegemite regularly have been found to be less stressed and anxious, so that's a ripper reason to put Vegemite on the top of your list if it's not already there. While my son, Harvey, jokes he has 'vegemititus' because he eats so much of it (as well as in his sandwich, he loves it stirred through spaghetti with a knob of butter and grated cheese, and smeared on top of a roast potato!) there are plenty of alternative fillings to have fun with. We've put our favourites together in this chapter to encourage some adventure beyond cheese and tomato.

And it was Its high concentration of B vitamins and other nutrients that helped Vegemite become a staple in soldiers' ration packs during World War II.

Is it contagious?

Note that the food guides in the following pages apply to the fillings, not your choice of bread.

AVOCADO AND . . .

egg-free / gluten-free (option)

Vegemite, olive tapenade (see recipe page 81) or anything, really! Place a piece of multi-grain toast on a plate then add a generous layer of smashed avo mixed with lemon juice, salt and pepper. Top with a dollop of ricotta, half a handful of roughly chopped toasted almonds, some pomegranate seeds, edible flowers or a combo of chopped mint and parsley, and you've got yourself an Instagrammable open sandwich! Too good to eat? Nah!

Is that even a word?

SAY CHEESE . . .
AND VEGEMITE!

egg-free / gluten-free (option) / nut-free / grain-free (option) / wheat-free (option)

Choose a mild cheese like colby, mozzarella or swiss which will complement the salty Vegemite taste. Spread a layer of Vegemite on one slice of bread then top with your chosen cheese, grated or thinly sliced. Place another layer of bread on top and it's good to go. Better still, pop the assembled sanga in a sandwich press for a few minutes until the cheese has melted and the bread is golden brown.

EGGSELLENT

You went there – again!

nut-free / gluten-free (option) / dairy-free / grain-free
(option) / wheat-free (option)

In a small bowl, gently mash two soft-boiled eggs
using a fork. Add some cracked black pepper, salt and a
tablespoon of mayonnaise (homemade, ideally). Spread
this mixture on one slice of your chosen bread. Can be
eaten as is or, for some crunch, add some iceberg lettuce,
mung bean sprouts and alfalfa sprouts – all of which are
loaded with goodness. Top with a second slice of bread.

Sprouts are little nutritional
powerhouses because they
contain a concentrated
number of nutrients to help
the shoot grow into an adult
plant. Vitamins A, C and K, for
example, as well as minerals
like calcium and magnesium,
can be found within these
small germinated seeds.

GREMOLATA

dairy-free / egg-free / gluten-free (option) /
grain-free (option) / wheat-free

A simple, raw Italian condiment that can jazz up many a
dish and is wonderful as a sandwich spread. Per person,
process ¼ cup (25 g) walnuts, ¼ cup flat-leaf parsley
leaves, 2 tablespoons lemon juice and 1 tablespoon
olive oil in a small food processor until well combined.
Season with salt and pepper and spread this mixture on
one slice of your chosen bread with a second slice on
top. Can be eaten as is or with added fillings like lettuce
or baby spinach leaves. Walnuts are brain food, olive
oil lubricates the joints, parsley contains vitamin C and
lemon juice aids the absorption of the vitamin C! You can
double or triple these quantities to make more gremolata
than you need and store it in an airtight container in the
fridge for a few days, until the next round of sandwiches.

And they also contain
significant amounts of
alpha linolenic acid or ALA,
a type of omega-3 fatty acid
that helps prevent blood
clots and lowers the risk of
ischemic heart disease.

ABC NUTTER

dairy-free / egg-free / gluten-free (option) / grain-free (option) / wheat-free (option)

To date, there are 98 published research papers on the health effects of almonds (with 19 more in progress) – in particular their benefits for heart health, diabetes and weight management.

It's so easy to make your own nut butter. This one, made from almonds , brazil nuts and cashews, tastes like a decadent treat. To make the nut butter, soak 1 cup of an equal mix of the three nuts in water overnight, then drain and process in a food processor to achieve the desired consistency – smooth, crunchy or somewhere in between. If it's super thick, add a little water or oil – olive, coconut, macadamia or sunflower seed oils work well. This butter provides a brilliant plant-based protein hit for hungry kids and is packed full of essential fatty acids. For a toasty flavour, instead of soaking the nuts, simply place them on a baking tray and dry-roast at 180°C for 10 minutes or until a slightly darker shade, before processing.

RED PESTO

dairy-free / egg-free / gluten-free (option) / grain-free (option) / wheat-free (option)

Basil offers flavonoid phytochemicals called orientin and vicenin which act like antioxidants, travelling through the body and neutralising the damaging free radicals that destroy normally healthy cells.

I always make more pesto than needed at any one time so I have a ready supply in the fridge for later. In a food processor, blend together ½ cup (70 g) semi-dried tomatoes, ½ cup (80 g) macadamias or pine nuts, 5–10 basil leaves, ¼ cup (60 ml) olive oil, sea salt and a sprinkling of chilli powder. For a thinner consistency add a little more olive oil or a splash of lemon juice. Spread 1–2 tablespoons of pesto on one slice of your chosen bread, add lots of lettuce and sliced cucumber, top with a second slice of bread . . . and hey pesto!

ROASTED VEG

dairy-free / egg-free / nut-free / gluten-free (option) /
grain-free (option) / wheat-free (option)

In my opinion there is nothing more mouth-watering than
piling leftover roast veggies like pumpkin and red onion
into two bits of sourdough. Place the veggies on the
bread and gently press with a fork to make an even layer.
Place a second slice of bread on top. The wonderful
roasted flavours of the veggies – especially after a day
in the fridge – stand alone and don't need anything extra,
but you could add some fresh chopped parsley and
a little mint jelly.

TRAFFIC LIGHT WRAP

dairy-free (option) / egg-free / nut-free /
gluten-free (option) / grain-free (option) /
wheat-free (option)

Kids love the colours in this and a rolled-up wrap
makes a nice change from a typical sandwich. If you are
looking for a bread that is yeast-free and less doughy,
then you can't go past mountain bread.
It's great for when you need bread to make a quick
snack but want a lighter option. Spread mountain bread
with smashed avocado or ricotta cheese, then add
a thin layer of grated zucchini or chopped cucumber,
grated carrot and sliced red or yellow capsicum.
Season with salt and pepper then roll it up, folding
the ends in to stop everything falling out. And – GO!

QUESADILLA

egg-free / gluten-free (option) / nut-free /
grain-free (option) / wheat-free (option)

Corn tortillas make a fabulous gluten-free option. Preheat a large frying pan or a flat grill sandwich maker. In a bowl, mash ½ cup (100 g) drained and rinsed red kidney beans (or white beans, like butter beans or cannellini) using a potato masher or fork, then add 1–2 tablespoons grated cheese and some chopped spring onions (both white and green ends). You can also add a few chilli flakes and a sprinkling of chopped fresh coriander. Mix together. Spread over a tortilla, then place a second tortilla on top. Using a wide spatula, place the quesadilla in the pan and cook for 5 minutes, then carefully turn and cook for a few more minutes so both sides are crisp and golden. (If using a sandwich maker, both sides will cook simultaneously in the 5 minutes.)

Amongst other things, red kidney beans are a brilliant source of folate – a folate deficit is associated with a greater risk of depression. They also contain phosphorus, a mineral needed for the growth, maintenance and repair of all tissues and cells starting from infancy.

HAPPY HUMMUS

dairy-free / egg-free / gluten-free (option) /
grain-free (option) / wheat-free (option) / nut-free

Hummus, made from chickpeas and tahini, is a fantastic spread for sangas (see recipe page 72). Not only does it keep everything between the slices of bread, but it's also a nutritious blend of protein and complex carbohydrates. Hummus goes well with so many different ingredients but particularly with slices of cucumber, bean sprouts and baby spinach leaves.

SMASHED BANANA

dairy-free / egg-free / nut-free (option) /
gluten-free (option) / grain-free (option) /
wheat-free (option)

Using a fork, mash together 1 banana with 1 tablespoon
of tahini or peanut or almond butter, a drizzle of lemon
juice and a sprinkling of cinnamon. Sandwich between
2 slices of bread. This is a sweet sanga, which goes well
after dinner as a substantial dessert or after sport.

FRUIT SANDWICH

egg-free / grain-free (option) / nut-free (option) /
gluten-free (option) / wheat-free (option)

As well as being a fabulous snack in its own right, fruit
is underrated as a sandwich filler. I love a thin slice of
dark rye for this breakfast special but Harvey loves
our local artisan baker's fruit loaf, which I toast for
him before he starts the build! To make, spread your
bread with a soft, mild cheese like ricotta or cottage
cheese. Sprinkle with cinnamon or nutmeg along with
a teaspoon of LSA (linseed, sunflower seed and almond
mix) or hemp seeds for a protein hit, then top with your
child's favourite fruits. Some great combinations to try
are thin slices of granny smith apple and celery; thin
lengthwise slices of strawberries and banana rounds;
peeled orange rounds and mint leaves; and the colourful
combination of whole blueberries and raspberries.

RECIPE LIST

EDAMAME

CORN ON THE COB

BOILED EGG

VEGEMITE BROTH

HALOUMI OR SAGANAKI

FRUIT STICKS

MINI BAKED POTATO

ROASTED CHICKPEAS

CAN OF TOMATOES

TAMARI NUTS

CHICKPEA PANCAKE

SALT AND PEPPER COCONUT CHIPS

9

ONE
BIT
WONDERS

THERE'S NOTHING WORSE than opening the fridge or pantry door and feeling as though you're looking in Old Mother Hubbard's cupboard. Grrr.

But wait: instead of giving up hope and dashing to the snack aisle in the supermarket – which is full of products laden with sugar and trans fats – squint your eyes and, just like an optical illusion, something appears before your eyes. There's almost always something you can make with what you've got; it's just a matter of changing your focus slightly.

Often the right answer is the simplest one but we overlook it because it seems too obvious or too easy. That's why in this chapter we're going to show you how to make satisfying snacks using just one 'hero' ingredient. The secret lies in taking one key item and tricking it up a little. It's the best solution for those times between meals when you just need to come up with something straightforward and speedy that fills a gap and offers nourishment too. And these recipes will come in handy even when the kitchen's fully stocked, because it's often when we're faced with lots of choice that we don't make the most sensible decisions .

The ideas in this chapter are all very simple, but I have also provided some extra inspiration in case you're not restricted by time or ingredients and want to create something more substantial. In addition to the hero ingredients, I have assumed that you have some basic

Trans fats can cause mayhem for cholesterol levels. They also contribute to obstructed blood vessels and increase levels of inflammatory markers – in other words, they really spell trouble.

There is something in psychology called 'decision fatigue', which means the quality of the decisions we make after a long day's study or work can deteriorate – sometimes leading to unwise food choices, especially in the evening. The concept of 'one bit wonders' reduces the decisions required because the ingredients are minimal. What a relief!

supplies in your pantry to make these recipes such as salt and pepper, coconut oil, simple herbs and spices.

It's important to remember that simple, quick and easy snacks can provide plenty of nourishment. 'Not-Reality' shows on television and food posts and photos on social media can contribute to parents feeling pressure to produce extraordinary dishes – but don't.

And so, drum roll please, I present to you . . . The One Bit Wonders!

EDAMAME

dairy-free / egg-free / gluten-free /
nut-free / wheat-free

These green young soybeans in a pod provide a delicious protein hit and are the only vegetable to contain all nine essential amino acids. In Australia we find this Japanese vegetable in the freezer section of most supermarkets. If not, consider taking a trip to a specialty store and stocking up. There is always a packet in my freezer and I replace it as soon as I run out.

Edamame are quick to cook – simply plunge the frozen pods into a saucepan of boiling water, bring back to the boil, and continue to boil for 3 minutes. Drain and plunge into cold water to prevent them from cooking further and to make them easier to handle, then peel and eat.

Edamame are delicious served warm straight from the pod without anything else added to them, or they can be served cold with salt and garlic flakes. If you put the cooled pods in a bowl in the centre of the table, everyone can pod and eat them. The process of peeling or podding the edamame helps to make the whole eating experience more mindful.

If your child doesn't like mature soybeans or tofu, don't worry – they're more likely to love edamame as they have a sweet, fresh taste and a lovely texture.

Yum! They're also naturally gluten-free and cholesterol-free, and rich in iron and calcium.

And delaying gratification makes you a better student. Do you remember me telling you about the marshmallow experiment in chapter 1? Delayed gratification is a major part of the self-regulation skills that enable kids to cope with change, both minor and major, later in life.

Healthy fast food! It really does exist!

CORN ON THE COB

dairy-free / egg-free / gluten-free /
grain-free / nut-free / wheat-free

Fresh corn is possibly the ultimate fast food. It can be cooked in the microwave in 3 minutes and on the stove in 5 minutes. If you're ever able to get your hands on corn picked straight from the stalk, do it! It's at its sweetest and juiciest then. Every hour after harvesting, the sugars turn to starches and change the taste. The best seasons for sweetcorn are summer and autumn, as this is when you can buy it fresh and cheap.

And the antioxidant activity of yellow corn actually appears to increase when you cook it! What's more, corn is packed with lutein and zeaxanthin, phytochemicals that foster healthy vision.

Stove-top instructions

1. Remove the husks and silks. Place corn into a saucepan of boiling water and bring the water back to the boil. Cover, turn off heat and sit corn in water for 5–7 minutes. Drain.

Microwave instructions

1. Place corn with husk intact in microwave and cook on HIGH (100 per cent) for 3 minutes. Using tongs or a tea towel, carefully remove from microwave as steam will be trapped inside. Cool slightly before removing the husk and silks.

Barbecue instructions

1. Fire up the barbecue. Dunk the corn with husk intact in a bowl of water for 1 minute. Place it on the barbecue and cook for 10–15 minutes, turning a couple of times. The husks will char and burn but once removed the corn will have a wonderful smoky flavour.

2. Serve seasoned with salt and pepper, or some parmesan cheese, or a little knob of butter with a sprinkling of chilli powder for some kick.

BOILED EGG

dairy-free / gluten-free / grain-free /
nut-free / wheat-free

In just 5 minutes you can conjure up a delicious and nutritious protein hit . Boiled eggs are a quick and easy snack to make and serve on the spot, or you can make these ahead of time so they are in the fridge ready and waiting for instant consumption! Boiled eggs last several days in the fridge.

Egg selection

I always choose organic free-range eggs because that's the closest to how my farming grandparents ate their eggs. There has been some debate around the quality and regulation of organic eggs and I know a lot of people who choose not to eat them, so my advice is to read up on egg production and the companies you are buying from so you can make an informed choice .

Egg storage

Always store eggs in their carton in the fridge.

Eggs must be one of the greatest memory foods going around: they're a marvellous source of choline, a crucial nutrient that's used to produce a neurotransmitter involved in memory, called acetylcholine. We tend to think of the yolk as the powerhouse, but did you know that more than 50 per cent of the protein of an egg is found in the white? Plus the white has lower amounts of fat and cholesterol than the yolk.

Alternatively, buy your eggs from a farmers' market or, if you have a backyard, think about getting your own chooks! There are companies that rent out the coop and the chooks to make it easy, and it means you can guarantee the source of your eggs.

Boiling eggs

1. If you have time, bring eggs to room temperature before cooking them to prevent the shells from cracking.

2. Place eggs in a saucepan and cover with cold water. Bring the water to the boil over medium–high heat, then reduce heat and keep at a simmer. For soft yolks simmer for 4–5 minutes; for firm yolks simmer for 8 minutes. If you want the egg to look perfect, stir the water in one direction during cooking as this will centre the yolk once cooked. Remove from heat and eat warm or write the date on the eggs, return to their carton and store in the fridge until needed.

3. An alternative method is to place the eggs in a saucepan and cover with cold water. Bring the water to the boil then turn off the heat, cover the pan and leave the eggs sitting in the hot water for 12 minutes. Why not give them both a go and see which way you like best!

4. Boiled eggs are complemented beautifully by a few generous grinds of salt and pepper and a little chopped parsley, or a teaspoon of mayonnaise with a sprinkling of curry powder. You can create an even more substantial snack by gently mashing them in between a couple of pieces of toast.

VEGEMITE BROTH

dairy-free / egg-free (option) / nut-free

About to run out of Vegemite? Make the most of what's left: save the 'empty' Vegemite jar and add hot (not boiling) water to the dregs, stir and drink! Or if you can't wait until the jar is empty, add 1 teaspoon Vegemite to a cup of hot water. It's vegetarian 'bone' broth! This is great on a winter's afternoon when the kids come running in from the cold and need warming up from the inside out. And for a Japanese alternative to Vegemite, try miso soup . It couldn't be easier to make: just add 1 teaspoon miso paste to a cup of hot but not boiling water. Stir and drink.

Flip, if there is 1 teaspoon left over in the jar of Vegemite, that provides half an adult's daily requirements for folate and thiamine – so good!

This is my all-time favourite! Miso is rich in essential minerals, vitamins B, E and K, and folate. It also feeds the gut with beneficial bacteria that help our gut health. They're now known to be linked to our overall mental and physical wellbeing!

For something more substantial:

1. Add 2 cups (500 ml) water to a small saucepan and bring to the boil. Reduce heat and keep at a simmer. Stir in 1–2 teaspoons miso paste and any or all of the following:
   - A small number of rice noodles
   - A handful of cubed tofu or tempeh
   - A few snow peas
   - Thinly sliced mushrooms
   - Chopped spring onions
   - 1 egg, beaten
2. Stir so the egg breaks up into ribbons. Simmer gently for 5 minutes or until everything has warmed through and the miso paste is mixed in. Top with some washed, chopped coriander.

HALOUMI OR SAGANAKI

egg-free / gluten-free / grain-free /
nut-free / wheat-free

These cheeses are high in protein and fat and low in carbohydrate – and if put in front of a hungry school kid who's just got home, they'll easily eat the lot ! To avoid this, I chop the haloumi into 1 cm-thick strips (which means you get about 6 rectangular strips per block) and put what I don't need back in the fridge. I generally allow 1 strip per person.

To make, warm a little olive oil in a small non-stick frying pan over high heat. Pan-fry the haloumi strips for 1 minute on each side or until golden brown. Chop into cubes, drizzle with lemon juice and serve.

For the saganaki, cook the block of cheese whole for 1 minute on both sides or until golden, remove from the pan and then chop into pieces. Drizzle with lemon juice and season with salt and pepper.

A word of warning from me: go easy on the cheese! Haloumi is also high in sodium, too much of which contributes to high blood pressure.[25] It's easy to overeat cheese, nuts and dips, so watch portion sizes. Anything larger than what you can hold in the palm of your hand is too much of these foods.

FRUIT STICKS

dairy-free / egg-free / gluten-free /
grain-free / nut-free / wheat-free

Gather whatever fruit is left in the fruit bowl or fridge, chop into bite-sized pieces and thread onto a skewer. Why? Because everything tastes better on a stick! Perhaps it's simply the different colours of the fruit on the stick that brightens our day . . . or that the bite-sized pieces are easier to tackle! With younger kids, in particular, offering them less familiar fruits in a creative way is a good method of introducing more variety. Try putting unfamiliar fruits in between fruity favourites to encourage their consumption.

To make, chop fruits like bananas and kiwi into 2 cm rounds; chop apples, plums, peaches and pears into bite sizes; leave grapes, blueberries and strawberries whole. Watermelon and cantaloupe can be chopped into cubes, or use a melon baller to create perfect spheres. Thread onto bamboo skewers or icy pole sticks. If you have some mint leaves, place these between the fruits. Be sure to blunt the sharp end before offering skewers to little kids and supervise them while they are eating.

Eat straight away or cover and chill in the fridge to eat later. These are also brilliant to use as dippers for the Chocolate Dip (see recipe page 82).

MINI BAKED POTATO

dairy-free (option) / egg-free / gluten-free /
grain-free / nut-free / wheat-free

In 2016, a Victorian man called Andrew Taylor came up with an unusual approach to tackling his addiction to food: he only ate potatoes for the whole year. And he lost 50 kg ! While I would never advocate such an extreme diet based solely on one ingredient, it does suggest that the sometimes maligned spud is more nutritious than you'd think, and that it's probably what you cook it in or slather on top that's the unhealthy part. Potato fries are a typical fast food, but maybe we can think of the whole spud as a *healthy* fast food. To keep portions for kids to a snackable size, use baby potatoes (sometimes called chats), which are ready in just a couple of minutes.

He also claimed it significantly reduced his depression and anxiety, helped him sleep better, improved his mental clarity, and lowered his cholesterol and blood pressure. But wouldn't you get sick of spuds?!

1. To make, pierce 1 or 2 potatoes all over with a fork or skewer. Place on a plate in the microwave and cook on HIGH (100 per cent) according to weight – 100 g of potato needs approximately 1.5 minutes. Sweet potatoes can also be cooked like this.
2. Halve potatoes, then add a little dollop of butter or a drizzle of olive oil, salt and pepper, and away you go. Homemade tomato sauce or a few shavings of parmesan cheese are delicious toppings, too. For sweet potatoes, drizzle with a little coconut oil and cinnamon or ginger.

TIP: To really amp up your cooked spuds, try adding some minty mushy green peas, Tapenade (see recipe page 81) with cherry tomatoes and rocket (arugula), Corn Salsa (see recipe page 76) or Gremolata (see recipe page 143).

ROASTED CHICKPEAS

dairy-free / egg-free / gluten-free /
nut-free / wheat-free

Chickpeas make a delicious snack simply roasted
with salt and pepper but they also work well with lots
of different flavours. So, grab some garam masala,
dukkha, mild chilli powder, garlic granules or any
other spice mix that's in the cupboard and experiment!
Roasted chickpeas store well so make a big batch and
keep them in an airtight container in the cupboard
for crunching on instead of store-bought chips.

Makes about 1½ cups

These lovely little legumes have been scientifically proven to increase satiety, in other words feelings of fullness – making them perfect for keeping the kids going between meals.

1 tablespoon olive oil
sea salt and ground black
   pepper
1 tablespoon dried
   rosemary

400 g canned chickpeas,
   rinsed and drained

1. Preheat the oven to 180ºC. Line a baking tray with
   baking paper.
2. Put the olive oil, several grinds of salt and pepper and
   the rosemary (or garam masala, dukkha, spice mix, garlic
   granules, chilli powder, etc.) in a bowl and stir to combine.
   Add the chickpeas and stir until evenly coated.
3. Spread the chickpeas over the lined tray and bake
   for 30 minutes or until golden. Stir or shake the tray
   occasionally to ensure the chickpeas are cooking evenly.
   For crunchier, more golden chickpeas, cook for 5 minutes
   longer.
4. Allow to cool a little before eating. Can be eaten cold too.

CAN OF TOMATOES

dairy-free / egg-free / gluten-free /
grain-free / nut-free / wheat-free

This has saved me many a time when the cupboard is almost bare and Harvey's dinner is still far from ready! This is NOT canned tomato soup, which often has a longer list of extras than *Neighbours* – this is a can of diced or whole tomatoes .

To make, simply empty the contents into a small saucepan and warm gently for about 5 minutes. Season with salt and pepper. Add some fresh basil leaves if you have them or, if you don't, ½ teaspoon of dried oregano. A few shakes of the chilli jar is an easy way to add more flavour. Add 1–2 cups water to create a bigger serve. Once warmed through, transfer to a bowl or cup, or blitz using a stick blender for a smoother, lighter texture. Stir through some Roasted Chickpeas (opposite) for a protein hit and delicious bite. If you have any leftover cooked penne pasta, some Cauliflower Bliss Bombs (see recipe page 97) or some baby spinach, stir any or all of these through for a mini minestrone. I often eat this for a simple lunch or late-night dinner.

Tomatoes are the best source of the carotenoid pigment lycopene, which may play a role in the prevention of prostate, lung and stomach cancers.[26] Tomatoes are better for you when heated, as lycopene is absorbed better when it has been cooked.

TAMARI NUTS

dairy-free / egg-free / gluten-free /
grain-free / wheat-free

You can make these on the spot and have a delicious ready-to-eat snack in 15–20 minutes or you can make a big batch every couple of weeks and keep them in a glass jar in the fridge to enjoy whenever hunger strikes. They're also a great way to use up nuts that have been on the shelf for a smidge too long! Both the Heart Foundation and Nutrition Australia recommend a daily serve of 30 g or a small handful of raw nuts and seeds. If making a big batch of tamari nuts, you can also portion them into small handfuls (approximately 30 g) and put them in zip lock bags in the freezer to prevent overeating them. Nuts don't actually freeze so you can pull them out of the freezer and eat straight away!

Nuts are truly heroic: a great source of vitamins B1, B2, B3 and E, beneficial mono and polyunsaturated oils PLUS calcium, iron, copper, magnesium, manganese and zinc. Phew!

I use equal portions of nuts – cashew, pecans, almonds, walnuts and brazil nuts – but just choose the nuts that your family loves. And while seeds are delicious, they are a bit fiddly to eat so I don't usually use them for this snack. If you do want to roast both nuts and seeds, put them on separate trays because they cook at different rates, and pull the seeds out earlier so they don't burn.

Especially good advice if you want to avoid meeting the men and women of your local fire brigade!

I've used tamari instead of soy sauce here because I prefer its milder taste, and it is gluten-free, which means this recipe is suitable for coeliacs like my husband.

1. To make, place the nuts and tamari into a bowl and stir so the nuts are coated in tamari. For every cup of nuts, use 1 tablespoon tamari. If you have time, allow to stand for 20 minutes for the flavour to develop.
2. Preheat the oven to 180°C. Line a baking tray with baking paper.
3. Spread the nuts over the lined tray and roast for 10–15 minutes. (Don't cook nuts at too high a heat or for too long otherwise their nutritional value is compromised.)
4. Allow to cool a little before eating or cool completely before transferring to an airtight container to store.

TIP: For another flavour option instead of tamari, add 1 teaspoon of garlic flakes and a pinch of cayenne pepper to the nuts before roasting.

CHICKPEA PANCAKE

dairy-free (option) / egg-free / gluten-free /
nut-free / wheat-free / freezable

Chickpea or besan flour is unlike many other flours: it's
gluten-free for starters, plus it is packed full of protein
and fibre and it has a lovely nutty, earthy taste. Chickpea
flour pancakes have a texture that's dense but not heavy,
especially if you make them thin, which I recommend.

For a spicy pancake: add ½ teaspoon dukkha or
garam masala to the mixture before cooking.

For a vegetable pancake: add ¼ cup finely chopped
red capsicum, some peas and corn to the mixture
before cooking.

Makes 1 thin pancake

½ cup (75 g) chickpea flour
½ cup (125 ml) water
sea salt and ground
   black pepper

1 teaspoon butter,
   ghee or oil

1. Put the chickpea flour and water in a small bowl and stir
   until well combined. Season with a pinch of salt and a
   few grinds of pepper. The mixture should have a smooth,
   pourable consistency. If you are using any herbs, spices
   or veggies, add them now.
2. Heat a small non-stick frying pan over low heat. Add the
   butter (or ghee or oil). Pour in the chickpea mixture and
   cook for 5 minutes or until the underside is golden in
   colour. Flip the pancake and cook for another 3 minutes
   or until golden. Serve warm.

SALT AND PEPPER COCONUT CHIPS

dairy-free / egg-free / gluten-free / grain-free / nut-free / wheat-free

These are so delicious and you can add a variety of flavours: my favourite is salt and pepper. Be sure to use coconut flakes for this recipe rather than shredded or desiccated coconut as they have a greater surface area to carry the flavours and are easier to eat – like a mini chip!

Makes about 1 cup

1 tablespoon coconut oil, melted
1 cup (50 g) coconut flakes

Flavour options:
½ teaspoon ground cinnamon
1 tablespoon sesame seeds
½ teaspoon ground ginger and ¼ teaspoon ground turmeric
¼ teaspoon chilli powder
2 tablespoons white vinegar and several very generous grinds of salt

1. Preheat the oven to 180°C. Line a baking tray with baking paper.
2. Put the coconut oil and whatever flavours you want in a medium-size bowl and stir to combine. Add coconut flakes and stir until the flakes are evenly coated.
3. Spread the coconut mixture evenly over the lined tray. Bake for 5–10 minutes or until light golden (keep a close eye on the clock). The salt and vinegar mix needs to be cooked for 15 minutes to get a crunch due to the vinegar, but check regularly to ensure the flakes don't brown or burn. Set aside to cool completely before serving.

RECIPE LIST

PAPER BAG POPCORN

DESK MIX

COCONUT CRUMBLES

CHEERY RIPES

BOUNTEE BITES

CHOCOLATE BARK

VENUS BARS

ALMOND BUTTER BARS

BANANA OAT BITES

BROWNIES

STRAWBERRY CHIA POTS

HONEYED WALNUTS

10

SMART
SWEET
THINGS

SUGAR IS A HIGHLY PROCESSED product that comes in numerous forms: white sugar, brown, raw, cane, caster, coconut, icing and granulated, plus brown sugars including muscovado, demerara, rapadura . . . Then there's the sugar in syrups such as honey, molasses, maple syrup and rice malt syrup. Not forgetting the naturally forming sugars in fruit.

So is there a good sugar? And what's the difference between glucose, fructose and sucrose? If it's natural, then surely it's okay . . . And if it has a low GI, is it okay? Is brown sugar better than white? And what about sugar-free sweeteners like stevia?

Confused? Don't worry. You are not alone.

Unlike in the UK, where a sugar tax on soft drinks has been introduced, policy makers in Australia still seem hesitant to bite the bullet despite the fact that soft drinks have no nutritional value. A 600 ml bottle of soft drink contains 16 teaspoons of sugar and about 1000 unnecessary kilojoules. We know that excess kilojoules can lead to weight gain and obesity. At the time of writing, an estimated 20–25 per cent of children and adolescents in Australia are overweight and a quarter of this group is obese.[27]

There are countless books, movies and organisations committed to educating us about our sugar consumption to help us make informed choices. There's lots to read and digest. Wherever you sit in the big sugar debate, there is no doubt that we are eating considerably more added sugar (not naturally occurring in milks, fruit and veg) these days than previous generations did. While the World Health Organization recommends adults limit our daily consumption of added sugar to 6–9 teaspoons and fewer than 6 teaspoons for children, according to the Australian Bureau of Statistics, in 2011–12 the average Australian consumed a whopping 14 teaspoons of white sugar each day.

If you limit all the obvious things like chips, sweets, chocolates, flavoured yoghurts, fruit drinks, soft drinks, tomato sauce and sweet cereals from your child's diet you'll be well on the way to reducing their processed sugar intake. It's as simple as reading the label. If it's a natural food like a piece of fruit that doesn't have a label, even better!

But sweet things don't need to be completely ruled out of a healthy diet – you just have to be smart about it. Choose naturally sweet snacks that are nutritionally sound and release energy slowly.

Apparently, 51 per cent of us have a 'sweet tooth', and I do love a sweet treat. I have created lots of delicious smart sweet snacks to fill that gap so I never feel like I am missing out.

To make my snacks sweet I utilise the naturally sweet flavours of bananas, dates, sweet potato, cinnamon, vanilla and coconut in its various forms. I also use nuts, cacao and coconut oil – all of which contain lots of good fats which help create satiety. Using these alternative ingredients means that you and your kids are no longer going up and down on the sugar-powered rollercoaster.

This chapter contains twelve ideas to get you going, including modern versions of old school favourites like my Venus Bars (see recipe page 176), Cheery Ripes (see recipe page 172) and Coconut Crumble (see recipe page 171). Paper Bag Popcorn (see recipe page 169) is, I reckon, one of the world's fastest and cheapest snacks to prepare and is a guaranteed winner. Desk Mix (see recipe page 170) tweaks the original trail mix. The six different tastes and textures from the ingredients, including goji berries and cacao nibs, make it a brilliant snack on which to nibble.

Most of the other recipes are just a matter of tossing a few ingredients into a food processor, pressing the mixture into a tray or rolling it into balls, and then chilling in the fridge for about 30 minutes before serving. Meanwhile, the Banana Oat Bites (see recipe page 179) and Brownies (see recipe page 180) need to be baked for 30 minutes. These are best made ahead of time. The good news is that all these recipes store well for several days in the fridge and even longer in the freezer, so the time spent making a few batches of them can set you up with a lasting supply.

Strawberry Chia Pots (see recipe page 182) are quick and easy to prepare but need time to chill in the fridge overnight. They're worth waiting for, though.

When making changes to my son's diet, my approach is to move slowly, steadily and quietly. I don't announce that changes are afoot. I introduce new things surreptitiously and scrumptiously. Old foods get dropped out of rotation, and the new food is drip-fed in!

If your kids have a sugary, fatty or salty snack you'd rather they didn't eat but that they are not willing to give up, don't worry. Keep it there. You don't need to win every food fight. I say, let them have a 'win' and allow them to enjoy it. Maybe just reduce the frequency it's eaten; then they will appreciate it even more when they do have it. Another approach is to bring the snack debate to the table. Get it out in the open. Talk to your kids about it. Explain why you want to make changes and encourage them to adopt them. Together you can do a stocktake of the snacks bought each week and get them to choose which ones go, and which ones in this book they would like to try. Slowly but surely, you can replace some, most or all the snacks they don't need with these delicious and nutritious alternatives.

PAPER BAG POPCORN

dairy-free / egg-free / gluten-free /
nut-free / wheat-free

Homemade popped corn is best eaten warm. It's perfect
as a *little* something to gnaw on shortly before dinner
or as an after-dinner snack. I reckon popped corn is
the cheapest snack in the world, with 1 tablespoon of
corn making 1 cup of popped corn, which is a generous
serve. It's one of the fastest snacks to whip up and you
can leave it plain or add a flavour. A packet of popping
corn lasts for ages in the cupboard – as do brown
paper bags – so they are both always in my pantry.

Popcorn was first discovered by native North Americans.
Imagine their surprise the first time a corn kernel 'popped'
and exploded into a little white flower from the bonfire!

Makes 2 cups

2 tablespoons popping
corn
1 paper bag (about
19 cm × 24 cm)

Optional flavours – ground
cinnamon, desiccated
coconut, sea salt, chilli
powder

1. Put the popping corn into the paper bag. Fold the open
   end of the bag over three times to enclose, then fold in the
   corners. (Don't use staples as the microwave will spark.)
2. Put the paper bag in the microwave and cook on HIGH
   (100 per cent) for 2 minutes. Carefully remove paper bag
   from microwave and open it, avoiding your face.
3. Add any additional flavours you like to the paper bag.
   Shake to coat popcorn evenly. Serve warm or cold.

DESK MIX

dairy-free / egg-free / gluten-free /
grain-free / wheat-free

You know trail mix? Well, I've designed this mix for
those of us who get stuck at our desks and would like
something to nibble on. Tiger nuts are not nuts at all
but actually a small root vegetable. They are gluten-,
nut- and dairy-free and full of resistant starch, which
aids digestion and lowers blood sugar levels. They are
extremely high in fibre, vitamins C and E, calcium, iron,
magnesium, zinc, potassium and good fats. Tiger nuts
are available at health food shops and online – they're
not in many supermarkets yet but are definitely worth
seeking out. Goji berries are sometimes called 'happy
berries' and have long been used in Chinese medicine.
They contain beta-carotene which can help your
vision – perfect for students who can't see the facts!
They are also packed with loads of other good things.

Makes about 2¼ cups

½ cup (50 g) walnuts
½ cup (70 g) tiger nuts (you
  can use either peeled
  or unpeeled but I prefer
  unpeeled)
¼ cup (30 g) goji berries
½ cup (25 g) shaved

coconut (sometimes
  called coconut chips
  or flakes)
¼ cup (40 g) pepitas
  (pumpkin seeds)
¼ cup (30 g) cacao nibs

These contain a powerful
phytochemical not found
in any other fruit!

1. Mix all ingredients in a large jar. I like to then divide up the
   mix into zip lock bags for portioned snacks.

**TIP: Desk Mix will keep for up to 2–3 weeks in an airtight
container or jar in the fridge.**

COCONUT CRUMBLES

dairy-free / egg-free / gluten-free /
grain-free / nut-free / wheat-free

My dad loved a Golden Rough (a coconut mixture covered in chocolate) as a special treat on Sunday nights after dinner , so I was wondering if my version would cut the mustard with him. It did, so with Dad's stamp of approval they made it here! Grab a couple of egg rings to create the perfect Golden Rough shapes.

Makes about 12

½ cup (40 g) desiccated coconut
½ cup (40 g) shredded coconut
½ cup (25 g) flaked coconut
¼ cup (25 g) cacao powder

¼ cup (30 g) cacao nibs (or goji berries)
1 tablespoon coconut sugar (optional)
½ cup (110 g) coconut oil, melted

Flip, this may explain your psychological stability – psychologists love a family ritual or tradition. The more rituals, the better children do in life! In fact, many researchers have found an association between family meal frequency and better academic performance, reduced substance abuse and better behaviour.

1. Line a large baking tray with baking paper.
2. Put all ingredients into a large bowl and stir until evenly mixed.
3. Place an egg ring on the lined tray. Spoon enough of the coconut mixture into the egg ring to fill it. Gently push mixture down with the back of a spoon. Carefully remove egg ring and repeat to make 12 rounds in total. (If you don't have egg rings, draw 7 cm-diameter circles on the baking paper to help you create the same sized shapes.)
4. Cover and chill in the fridge until set. Serve.

TIP: Coconut Crumbles will keep for up to 1 week in an airtight container in the fridge.

CHEERY RIPES

dairy-free / egg-free / gluten-free /
grain-free / wheat-free

Okay, confession time . As a teenager, I probably ate my body weight in Cherry Ripes each year. But this homemade version makes me feel even more cheery than the original because it uses considerably less sugar.

Makes about 36

Take a seat on my couch!

Fact: they are the oldest chocolate bars to be produced in 'stralia and for a few years were by far the most popular. In 2012–13, believe it or not 10 per cent of Aussies ate at least one every month!

C is for cranberries, as well as the vitamin C they contain that can help to maintain healthy skin, blood vessels, bones and cartilage. Their vitamin K content helps wounds heal properly and is important for healthy bones, too.

1 cup (140 g) sweetened dried cranberries
2 cups (140 g) shredded coconut
2 cups (300 g) unsalted raw cashews
¼ cup (60 g) coconut oil, melted
pinch of sea salt
1 teaspoon vanilla extract

For the chocolate topping:
¼ cup (60 g) coconut oil, melted
¼ cup (25 g) cacao powder, sifted
1 tablespoon maple syrup (optional)

1. Line the base and sides of a 16 cm × 26 cm (base measurement) roasting tin with baking paper.
2. Put the dried cranberries, coconut, cashews, coconut oil, sea salt and vanilla into a food processor and process until well combined.
3. Transfer the mixture into the lined tin and gently press into all corners. Place in the fridge or freezer for about 30 minutes or until set. Remove the tray from the fridge or freezer and cut into pieces of your desired size.
4. To make the chocolate topping, simply put all the ingredients into a medium bowl and stir until well combined.

5. The slice tastes delicious without the chocolate layer so don't feel you need to add it if you're short on time, but to replicate the traditional Cherry Ripe . . . dip each piece into the chocolate mixture and transfer to a lined tray.
6. Refridgerate (or freeze) for 30 minutes until the ganache has set before serving.
7. Store for up to 1 week in an airtight container in the fridge, or the freezer for longer (but they never last that long at our place!).

TIP: Instead of dried cranberries you can also use dried cherries, softened goji berries or a mixture. This recipe works just as well with other dried fruits like apricots and prunes, too.

BOUNTEE BITES

dairy-free / egg-free / gluten-free /
grain-free / nut-free / wheat-free

Bounty bars, which have been around since 1951, are the inspiration behind these Bountee Bites.

Makes 24 bites or 12 bars

Coconut oil is super high in natural saturated fats, which increase both good (HDL) and bad (LDL) cholesterols.

1 cup (250 ml) canned coconut cream

4 cups (320 g) desiccated coconut (this works better than shredded or flaked)

2 tablespoons maple syrup

2 tablespoons coconut oil, melted

For the chocolate coating:
1 cup (220 g) coconut oil, melted

1 cup (100 g) cacao powder

2 tablespoons maple syrup

1. Line the base and sides of a 16 cm × 26 cm (base measurement) roasting tin with baking paper or foil.

2. Put the coconut cream, desiccated coconut, maple syrup and coconut oil into a large bowl. Stir until well combined and moist. If not moist enough, add a little extra coconut oil.

3. Transfer mixture into the lined tin so it's about 2 cm deep, press into the corners and smooth the top with a spatula. Cover and pop in the freezer for 30 minutes or until set.

4. Once the mixture is set, slice into 24 bite-sized pieces, or 8 rectangular bars.

5. To make the chocolate coating, put the coconut oil, cacao powder and maple syrup into a shallow bowl and combine.

6. Line a large baking tray with baking paper. Dip bites into chocolate and transfer to lined tray. Pop in the fridge for 10 minutes for the coating to harden before serving.

CHOCOLATE BARK

dairy-free / egg-free / gluten-free /
grain-free / nut-free / wheat-free

This is quick and easy to make and is perfect when
the need for something sweet sneaks up.
If you want to amp this up, before freezing evenly
sprinkle some of the following combos across
the mixture: pistachio and cranberries; shredded
coconut and dried strawberries; flaked almonds and
pumpkin seeds; or goji berries and cacao nibs.

1 cup (220 g) coconut oil
¼ cup (25 g) cacao powder

1 teaspoon ground
cinnamon

1. Line a 16 cm × 26 cm (base measurement) roasting tin
   with baking paper.
2. Melt the coconut oil in a small saucepan over low heat.
   Add cacao powder and cinnamon and stir until well
   combined.
3. Pour the mixture into the lined tin and spread to an even
   thickness. Sprinkle with whatever ingredients you love:
   my favourite combo is flaked coconut, goji berries and
   pumpkin seeds because it looks so colourful and
   is delicious. Pop into the freezer for 20 minutes.
4. Break into 'bark' – random shapes and sizes.

TIP: Chocolate Bark will keep for a couple of weeks
in the fridge and longer in the freezer (but it never
lasts that long at our place!). Bountee Bites (opposite)
will keep for up to 1 week in an airtight container in the
fridge, or freezer for longer.

VENUS BARS

dairy-free / egg-free / gluten-free / wheat-free

This is the reimagined Mars bar, which has layers of chocolate, choc-malt nougat and caramel. The Venus Bar has three layers and looks fabulous on the plate. Kids only need a small piece because it's so rich but it has lots of lovely different textures so they might have trouble stopping at one! This recipe calls for mesquite powder which is from a South American plant of the same name. You do need to make a trip to the heath food store to get this. Mesquite powder is gluten-free and high in fibre, protein and other minerals including potassium, magnesium, zinc and iron. It has a sweet nutty taste and adds a lovely caramel flavour but the recipe won't fail if you don't have any.

Makes 30–36

Buckwheat has a sweet flavour. It's good for cleaning and strengthening the intestines as it has a high level of fibre, which adds bulk to bowel movements, aiding movement through the gastrointestinal tract.

Caramel layer
1½ cups (285 g) buckwheat
1½ cups (270 g) pitted medjool dates (about 13)
1–2 tablespoons mesquite powder (optional)

Choc-malt nougat layer
3 cups (450 g) raw unsalted cashews
⅓ cup (75 g) coconut oil, melted

½ cup (50 g) cacao powder
1 tablespoon rice malt syrup

Chocolate layer
½ cup (125 ml) canned coconut milk
¼ cup (60 g) coconut oil, melted
1 tablespoon cacao powder
1 tablespoon maple syrup
1 teaspoon vanilla extract

1. To make the caramel layer, put the buckwheat into a food processor and process until ground, but still with texture.

2. Add the dates and mesquite powder (if using) and process again until well combined and the mixture comes together.

3. Line a 16 cm × 26 cm (base measurement) roasting tin with baking paper. Press the buckwheat mixture into the lined tin, pushing it into all the corners to make an even layer. I use my fingers for this as it's a dense but pliable mixture.

4. To make the choc-malt nougat layer, put the cashews, coconut oil, cacao powder and rice malt syrup into the food processor and process until well combined. (Don't worry about cleaning the food processor between these steps.) Press this mixture on top of your 'caramel' layer. Again, try and get it as evenly spread as possible; I find fingers are the best tools for this task.

5. For the third and final chocolate layer, put the coconut milk, coconut oil, cacao powder, maple syrup and vanilla into a clean food processor or blender and process until well combined. Pour over the top of the other layers to evenly cover. Chill in the fridge or freezer for 1 hour or until set.

6. This layer will have a lovely mousse-like consistency so it will be soft to the touch even after refrigeration. Cut into pieces to serve.

TIP: Venus Bars will keep for up to 3–5 days in an airtight container in the fridge.

ALMOND BUTTER BARS

dairy-free / egg-free / gluten-free /
grain-free / wheat-free

**This is decadent and delicious, and probably
club house leader for snacks!**

Makes 30 (but it depends how you slice it!)

Except, Flip, that almond
butter has an infinitely
superior nutritional profile
due to a favourable fat
content – and is kinder to the
heart as it is not high in salt!

½ cup (110 g) coconut oil
½ cup (140 g) almond butter
  (peanut butter or any
  other nut butter is also
  okay to use)
¼ cup (40 g) pepitas
  (pumpkin seeds)

¼ cup (35 g) sunflower
  seeds
¼ cup (30 g) goji berries
¼ cup (20 g) shredded
  coconut
sea salt

1. Line a 16 cm × 26 cm (base measurement) roasting tin
   with baking paper.
2. Put the coconut oil and almond butter into a small
   saucepan and warm, stirring, over a very low heat until
   well combined.
3. Add all the remaining ingredients and stir until everything
   is well covered.
4. Pour the mixture into the lined tin and, using a spoon,
   push the mixture into the corners to ensure you have
   created an even slab.
5. Place in the freezer for 20 minutes or until firm.
   Cut into bars.

**TIP: Almond Butter Bars will keep for a couple of weeks
in the fridge and longer in the freezer. Banana Oat
Bites (opposite) will keep for up to 1 week in an airtight
container in the fridge.**

BANANA OAT BITES (A.K.A. BOBS)

dairy-free / egg-free / nut-free / wheat-free

Many muesli bars or slices are loaded with sugar so these bites are a great alternative . Despite looking like a biscuit, these bites are not sweet and you might get a bit of a surprise when you first taste them. If you think you need more sweetness, add more maple syrup and then reduce it over time.

They're also high in fibre, good for feeling full for longer.

Makes about 15

3 very ripe medium-sized bananas, mashed
⅓ cup (100 g) stewed or puréed apple
¼ cup (40 g) currants
¼ cup (20 g) shredded coconut
1 teaspoon ground cinnamon
1 teaspoon vanilla extract
2–2½ cups (180–225 g) rolled (traditional) oats
1 tablespoon maple syrup (optional)

1. Preheat the oven to 180°C. Line a baking tray with baking paper.
2. Combine the bananas, apple, currants, coconut, cinnamon and vanilla in a large bowl. Add the oats and stir until well combined. Depending on the size and squishiness of the bananas, more or fewer oats may be needed to make a sticky but pliable mixture.
3. Roll the mixture into ping pong-sized balls and place on the lined tray. Use a fork to gently flatten the balls until they're about 1 cm thick.
4. Bake for 20–25 minutes or until starting to turn golden. Set aside to cool on the tray. Serve.

BROWNIES

dairy-free / gluten-free (option) / grain-free (option) /
nut-free / wheat-free (option)

I have many chocolate brownie recipes. Some use
avocado or black beans, while others are made with
almond meal, linseeds, desiccated coconut, dates
or walnuts. This one features sweet potatoes and
eggs – two ingredients Harvey doesn't like. Just don't
tell him what it's made of because he loves this recipe!
I use banana flour in this recipe as it is gluten-free
and I like the taste. Banana flour is traditionally made
from green bananas but doesn't actually taste of
banana – instead it has a mild earthy taste. It's also full of
resistant starch which is believed to have several health
benefits including lowering blood glucose levels.

Did you know green banana
flour is also abundant in
potassium – so much so that
just 2 tablespoons contain the
equivalent of 7 whole bananas!

Makes about 36

2 cups (250 g) grated sweet
   potato (about 1–2 sweet
   potatoes)
4 eggs
1 teaspoon vanilla extract
pinch of sea salt
1 teaspoon ground
   cinnamon
½ cup (50 g) cacao powder
½ cup (110 g) coconut oil,
   melted
¼ cup (60 ml) maple syrup
   or honey
¼ cup (35 g) banana or
   coconut flour (or ⅓ cup
   regular plain flour)

1 teaspoon bicarbonate
   of soda

Ganache (optional)
¼ cup (25 g) cacao powder
¼ cup (60 g) coconut oil,
   melted
1 tablespoon maple syrup
   (optional)

Topping
1 tablespoon cacao nibs
2 tablespoons coconut
   flakes
1 tablespoon goji berries
or ½ cup (75 g) fresh
   blueberries or raspberries

1. Preheat the oven to 180°C. Line a 16 cm × 26 cm (base measurement) roasting tin with baking paper.
2. To make the brownie, put all the ingredients into a large mixing bowl and stir until well mixed.
3. Spoon the mixture into the lined tin and spread evenly using the back of a spoon. Bake for 30 minutes. Cover the top of the brownie slab with foil and bake for 10 minutes further or until an inserted skewer comes out clean. Transfer the tin to a wire rack and leave to set for 10 minutes.
4. To make the ganache, put the cacao powder, coconut oil and maple syrup (if using) into a small bowl and stir until well combined.
5. Turn out the whole brownie slab on to a serving platter.
6. Drizzle ganache over the brownie, then sprinkle with cacao nibs, coconut flakes and goji berries – or fresh blueberries and raspberries.
7. Eat warm or put the brownie slab in the fridge for 20 minutes or until ganache has firmed.
8. Cut into pieces and serve.

TIP: Brownies will keep for up to 2–3 days in an airtight container in the fridge.

STRAWBERRY CHIA POTS

dairy-free (option) / egg-free / gluten-free /
grain-free / nut-free (option) / wheat-free

**These chia pots are very versatile. Not only are they a
super smart snack for morning or afternoon tea, but they
are also fabulous for a light breakfast when it's too early
to eat much or a late breakfast when lunch is not far away.
Oh, and they make a great dessert too!**

Makes 4

1 cup (150 g) chopped fresh
   strawberries (or any
   seasonal berries)
1 cup (250 ml) milk (almond,
   coconut or another
   nut milk, or 1 cup plain
   yoghurt and ricotta also
   works)

1 teaspoon vanilla extract
½ teaspoon ground
   cinnamon
2 tablespoons shredded
   coconut
⅓ cup (50 g) chia seeds
small handful (¼ cup) mint
   leaves, to serve

Chia seeds come from the
desert plant *Salvia hispanica*,
which is actually part of the
mint family. They're rich in
of omega-3 fatty acids – fats
that are crucial for heart
health and brain function.
And they're a whopping 34 per
cent fibre, which is more than
flaxseeds or sesame seeds.

1. Put the strawberries, milk, vanilla and cinnamon into a
   blender and blend until smooth. Stir in coconut.

2. Pour mixture into four 1-cup (250 ml) ramekins or glasses.
   Stir 1 tablespoon of the chia seeds into each ramekin.
   Cover with plastic film and pop in the fridge to chill
   overnight.

3. The next day, serve topped with a few mint leaves.

**TIP: Sometimes I prefer my Strawberry Chia Pots
to be less firmly 'set', especially if I am going to add
them to stewed apple or granola. For those times,
I use 2 teaspoons chia seeds per pot.**

HONEYED WALNUTS

dairy-free / egg-free / gluten-free /
grain-free / wheat-free

Walnuts go from wow to KAPOW with the addition of the winning combination of honey , vanilla and cinnamon. Be careful to watch portion size because these honeyed walnuts are so delicious it's easy to eat the entire serving in one go. The honey and spices get into all the nooks and crannies of the walnuts, but smooth almonds or cashews are a good alternative.

Makes 1 cup

1 cup (100 g) walnut halves
2 tablespoons honey

½ teaspoon vanilla extract
¼ teaspoon cinnamon

I always use pure honey from a reputable Australian supplier, to minimise the risk of it having been adulterated with bulking agents such as rice, beet, corn or wheat syrups, cheap sweeteners which can dilute honey's natural vitamin and mineral content.

1. Place a sheet of baking paper on a cooling rack.
2. Place all the ingredients in a small heavy-based saucepan and cook over a medium heat for 3 minutes, stirring continuously as honey caramelises and walnuts toast. Watch that the mixture or nuts don't burn.
3. Transfer the mixture to the lined cooling rack and allow to cool completely, about 30 minutes, before transferring to an airtight container lined with baking paper. Or eat warm.

TIP: Honeyed Walnuts are best kept for 1 week in an airtight container in the fridge, or for 1 month in the freezer.

ACKNOWLEDGEMENTS

Dr Michael Carr-Gregg: First of all I have to thank my fabulous foodie friend, Flip Shelton, for agreeing to come on this journey with me. It's been an epicurean adventure and I am indebted to you for your wisdom and patience. To Izzy Yates and Ali Watts, I am grateful for the care, kindness and skill you have both exhibited in helping us create this much-needed book. It is my eleventh book with Penguin Random House and when it comes to literary panel beaters, you are the best! Lastly to my wife, Therese, who taught me most of what I know about cooking, and our boys, Christopher and Rupert, who did most of the eating.

Flip Shelton: Thank you from the bottom of my heart to my wonderful co-author, MCG. Your wit and wisdom fantasticates my recipes perfectly. You are as serious as you are funny. As wise as a parliament of owls and so kind and generous of spirit. We started this book more than ten years ago, so it's glorious to see it realised. Thank you to Izzy Yates and Ali Watts. Publishing is a tough game with budgets and deadlines, restrictions and conditions. You made the jigsaw work and the end-result is a book I am so immensely proud of. I also consider myself incredibly lucky to be published by Penguin Random House. Thank you to my loyal, loving husband, Joffa, and divine son, Harvey. You two are my constant inspiration for the search and creation of delicious and nutritious food. You are also my toughest but most honest critics. Thanks to you, the reader, for buying this book. If you are at the start of your gastronomic journey, part way down the path or maybe motoring along the happy, healthy highway – I hope this book provides lots of ideas to effect positive change. If knowledge is power (a quote attributed to English philosopher, Sir Francis . . . er Bacon! in 1597), then food is powerful.

FURTHER READING

1. Australian Psychological Society Compass for life survey November 2016
2. http://www.abc.net.au/news/2016-03-21/australian-sugar-intake-remains-high-research/7263200
3. https://bmcmedicine.biomedcentral.com/articles/10.1186/s12916-015-0461-x
4. https://www.tandfonline.com/doi/full/10.1080/08870446.2017.1380813
5. https://www.oecd-ilibrary.org/social-issues-migration-health/society-at-a-glance-2009_9789264077904-ko
6. http://www.opc.org.au/downloads/policy-briefs/evidence-food-advertising-effects-children.pdf#.WMH6HRJ96T9
7. http://www.shopnaturally.com.au/stasher-reusable-bags.html
8. https://www.smh.com.au/articles/2003/01/23/1042911493790.html
9. https://www.smh.com.au/news/National/Year-12-students-at-risk-of-stress/2006/04/16/1145125991572.html
10. https://abcnews.go.com/Health/story?id=118266&page=1
11. https://doi.org/10.1002/9780470740668.ch8
12. https://www.ncbi.nlm.nih.gov/pubmed/20438265
13. http://journals.sagepub.com/doi/abs/10.1177/0956797614524581
14. https://ac.els-cdn.com/S0735109714015836/1-s2.0-S0735109714015836-main.pdf?_tid=6519b1d2-b1aa-424d-bc65-c0cf61df4e8b&acdnat=1531102532_f5ac11c9f8745e08a405e49c1810936a
15. http://www.viriya.net/jabref/the_relation_of_strength_of_stimulus_to_rapidity_of_habit-formation.pdf
16. https://allaboutbanana.wordpress.com/2013/06/10/what-does-a-banana-do-for-your-brain/)
17. http://www.wju.edu/about/adm_news_story.asp?iNewsID=1106&strBack=%2Fabout%2Fadm_news_archive.asp
18. http://europepmc.org/abstract/MED/24161892/reload=0;jsessionid=q05WWgGVo23tqRXunSYR.38
19. https://www.ncbi.nlm.nih.gov/pmc/articles/PMC3409373/
20. Martin I, *Aromatherapy for Massage Practitioners*. Lippincott Williams & Wilkins, Baltimore 2007 p.57

21. https://news.wfu.edu/2017/04/19/beetroot-juice-exercise-aging-brains-look-younger/

22. https://blog.totalwellbeingdiet.com/how-to-keep-your-gut-healthy

23. https://www.express.co.uk/life-style/health/316013/Avocado-hailed-as-new-anti-ageing-superfood

24. http://www.wju.edu/about/adm_news_story.asp?iNewsID=960&strBack=%2Fabout%2Fadm_news_archive.asp
AND
http://www.theintelligencer.net/news/community/2017/03/wju-looks-to-peppermint-its-effect-on-athletic-performance/

25. https://sodiumbreakup.heart.org/how_much_sodium_should_i_eat

26. https://www.sciencedirect.com/topics/biochemistry-genetics-and-molecular-biology/lycopene

27. https://www.healthdirect.gov.au/childhood-obesity-and-overweight-children

INDEX

A

ABC, 54
ABC nutter, 142
Açaí, 55
almonds
   ABC nutter, 142
   Almond butter bars, 178
   Gluten-free almond meal
      crackers, 85
   Gluten-free apricot balls, 42
   Matcha balls, 46–7
   Smoosli, 56
   Zesty coconut balls, 40
   Zucchini chips, 95
antioxidants, 36, 43, 46, 48, 65,
   74, 82, 83, 90, 129, 135, 142, 151
apples
   Apple sandwich, 118
   Banana oat bites
      (a.k.a. Bobs), 179
apps, 17, 27, 28, 125
apricots (dried)
   Apricot balls, 41
   Gluten-free apricot balls, 42
   Prune and walnut balls
      (a.k.a. 'Prunut balls'), 43
'Ave an avo, 116
avocados
   ABC, 54
   'Ave an avo, 116
   Avocado and . . . , 140
   Avocado chips, 90
   Avocado ice-creams
      (a.k.a. ice-vocados), 129
   Chocolate mousse, 103
   freezing, 53
   I pine for you, 57
   It's easy being green, 62

nutritional value, 73, 129
Simple guacamole, 73
Traffic light wrap, 143

B

Bagel crackers, 84
Baked bananas, 106
balls, 34–49
   Apricot balls, 41
   Banana balls, 39
   Cashew balls, 34–5, 37
   Chai-spiced sunflower
      seed balls, 38
   Chocolate coconut balls, 48
   Gluten-free apricot balls, 42
   Hemp seed balls, 44
   Hummus balls, 45
   Matcha balls, 46–7
   Oat balls, 36
   Prune and walnut balls
      (a.k.a. Prunut balls), 43
   Tahini balls, 49
   Zesty coconut balls, 40
bananas
   Baked bananas, 106
   Banana balls, 39
   Banana bites, 121
   Banana oat bites (a.k.a.
      Bobs), 179
   Bananarama ice-creams, 131
   Choconana, 59
   as late night snack, 100
   Smashed banana, 145
basil
   Red pesto, 142
   Tomato salsa, 77
beetroots
   Beet the bloat, 65

Beetroot, carrot and parsnip
   chips, 91
Get red(dy) and go, 66
nutritional value, 133
Up beet, 133
berries
   Berry good idea, 116
   Perfect parfait, 104
   Strawberry chia pots, 182
beta-amyloid, 55
beta-carotene, 62, 74, 82, 94,
   118, 170
Blanched greens, 120
blueberries
   ABC, 54
   Açaí, 55
   Fruitcicles, 128
   Happy water, 134
Boiled egg, 152–3
Bountee bites, 174
bread, 138–9
brown rice
   Brown rice, coconut oil
      and hemp seeds, 110
   time-saving tips, 21
Brownies, 180–1
buckwheat: Venus bar, 176–7

C

cabbage: Tummy tonic, 64
Cacao balls, 34–5
cacao nibs
   Caramel and choc chip
      ice-creams, 130
   Coconut crumbles, 171
   Desk mix, 170
cacao powder
   Banana balls, 39

Bountee bites, 174
Brownies, 180–1
Cacao balls, 34–5
Cheery ripes, 172–3
Chocolate bark, 175
Chocolate coconut balls, 48
Chocolate dip, 82
Chocolate mousse, 103
Choconana, 59
Coconut crumbles, 171
nutritional value, 48
Tahini balls, 49
Venus bar, 176–7
Can of tomatoes, 159
cantaloupe, 82
Caramel and choc chip
ice-creams, 130
cardamom, 61
carotenoid, 63, 83, 93
carrots
Beet the bloat, 65
Beetroot, carrot and parsnip
chips, 91
Roasted carrot dip, 74
Carskadon, Mary, 101–2
cashews, 79
ABC nutter, 142
Bananarama ice-creams, 131
Cashew balls, 37
Cheery ripes, 172–3
Choconana, 59
Matcha balls, 46–7
Venus bar, 176–7
Cauliflower bliss bombs, 97
cayenne pepper, 90
celery: Celery boats, 118
Chai-spiced sunflower seed
balls, 38
Cheery ripes, 172–3
cheese
Haloumi/Saganaki, 155
Say cheese . . . and Vegemite!
140
See also ricotta
chia seeds
Raspberry chia, 58

Strawberry chia pots, 182
chickpeas
Chickpea pancake, 162
Happy hummus, 144
Hummus balls, 45
Hummus in a hurry, 72
Roasted chickpeas, 158
chilli, 71
Chinese pudding, 119
chips
Avocado chips, 90
Beetroot, carrot and parsnip
chips, 92
Cauliflower bliss bombs, 97
Kale chips, 92
Polenta wedges, 93
Salt and vinegar chips
(sort of!), 96
Sweet potato fries, 94
Zucchini chips, 95
Chocolate bark, 175
Chocolate coconut balls, 48
Chocolate dip, 82
Chocolate mousse, 103
Choconana, 59
choline, 90, 120, 152
cinnamon, 43
coconut (dessicated), 36
Bountee bites, 174
Coconut crumbles, 171
coconut (flakes)
Coconut crumbles, 171
Desk mix, 170
Salt and pepper coconut
chips, 163
coconut (shredded)
Almond butter bars, 178
Apricot balls, 41
Banana balls, 39
Banana oat bites (a.k.a.
Bobs), 179
Cacao balls, 34–5
Cheery ripes, 172–3
Chocolate coconut balls, 48
Coconut crumbles, 171
Gluten-free apricot balls, 42

Matcha balls, 46–7
Prune and walnut balls
(a.k.a. 'Prunut balls'), 43
Zesty coconut balls, 40
coconut cream
Bountee bites, 174
Caramel and choc chip
ice-creams, 130
Coconut rice, 107
Perfect parfait, 104
Coconut crumbles, 171
coconut milk
Avocado ice-creams
(a.k.a. ice-vocados), 129
Chocolate mousse, 103
Coconut rice, 107
Mango and coconut
ice-creams, 127
Raspberry chia, 58
Satay dip, 80
Venus bar, 176–7
coconut oil
Bountee bites, 174
Brownies, 180–1
Chocolate bark, 175
Coconut rice, 107
coconut water, 55
ABC, 54
Fruitcicles, 128
Hit the tropics, 63
I pine for you, 57
coriander: Simple guacamole,
73
corn
Corn on the cob, 151
Corn salsa, 76
as late night snack, 100
Paper bag popcorn, 169
cortisol, 29
crackers
Bagel crackers, 84
Flatbread crackers, 83
Gluten-free almond meal
crackers, 85
cranberries (dried): Cheery ripes,
172–3

cucumber
  Get red(dy) and go, 66
  Happy water, 134
  It's easy being green, 62
  Kombucha 'juice', 67
  nutritional value, 132
  Tzatziki, 75
  Veggie poles, 132
curcumin, 37

D

dates See medjool dates
dates (fresh): Chocolate coconut
  balls, 48
decision fatigue, 148
Desk mix, 170
dips
  Chocolate dip, 82
  Corn salsa, 76
  Green pea dip
    (a.k.a. dippy), 78
  Happy hummus, 144
  Hummus in a hurry, 72
  Roasted carrot dip, 74
  Satay dip, 80
  Simple guacamole, 73
  Spinach and ricotta dip, 79
  Tapenade, 81
  Tomato salsa, 77
  Tzatziki, 75
  See also spreads
D.I.Y. yoghurt pot, 121
drinks, 17–18
  Happy water, 134
  Iced tea, 135
  Turmeric latte, 111
  See also fluid intake

E

Edamame, 150
eggs
  Boiled egg, 152–3
  Eggsellent, 141
  nutritional value, 120

Super-speedy egg, 120
time-saving and storing
  tips, 22
ellagic acid, 58
Ezekiel bread, 139

F

fast food
  Apple sandwich, 118
  'Ave an avo, 116
  Banana bites, 121
  Berry good idea, 116
  Blanched greens, 120
  Celery boats, 118
  Chinese pudding, 119
  D.I.Y. yoghurt pot, 121
  Make it a date, 117
  The Six Cs, 117
  Spinach soup, 119
  Super-speedy egg, 120
Fast Food Nation (Schlosser),
  88
fisetin, 132
Flatbread crackers, 83
flavonoid phytochemicals, 142
fluid intake, 16–18
folate, 61, 95, 118, 132, 144, 164
freezing tips, 20–1, 53
fruit
  freezing tips, 20–1, 53
  Fruit sandwich, 145
  Fruit sticks, 156
  Fruitcicles, 128
  Perfect parfait, 104

G

garlic: Tzatziki, 75
Get red(dy) and go, 66
ginger
  Beet the bloat, 65
  Happy water, 134
  Roasted carrot dip, 74
  Satay dip, 80
  Tummy tonic, 64

Gluten-free almond meal
  crackers, 85
Gluten-free apricot balls, 42
goji berries
  Almond butter bars, 178
  Desk mix, 170
Green pea dip (a.k.a. dippy),
  78
green tea, 135 See also
  Matcha balls
Gremolata, 141

H

Haloumi, 155
Happy hummus, 144
Happy water, 134
hemp seeds
  Brown rice, coconut oil
    and hemp seeds, 110
  Hemp seed balls, 44
Hit the tropics, 63
honey, 82
  Honeyed walnuts, 183
Hummus balls, 45
Hummus in a hurry, 72

I

I pine for you, 57
ice-creams/ icy poles
  Avocado ice-creams
    (a.k.a. ice-vocados), 129
  Bananarama ice-creams,
    131
  Caramel and choc chip
    ice-creams, 130
  Fruitcicles, 128
  Mango and coconut
    ice-creams, 127
  Up beet, 133
  Veggie poles, 132
  Watermelon and raspberry
    icy poles, 126
Iced tea, 135
It's easy being green, 62

J

juices
  Beet the bloat, 65
  Get red(dy) and go, 66
  Kombucha 'juice', 67
  Tummy tonic, 64

K

kale
  Get red(dy) and go, 66
  Kale chips,92
kefir: Zucchini and kefir, 60
kiwi fruit, 128
Kombucha 'juice,' 67

L

legumes See chickpeas; red
  kidney beans
linseeds, 59
L-theanine, 46, 135
lucuma powder: Caramel and
  choc chip ice-creams, 130
lycopene, 159

M

maca powder
  Hemp seed balls, 44
  Smoosli, 56
macadamias: Red pesto, 142
Make it a date, 117
mangoes
  Corn salsa, 76
  Fruitcicles, 128
  Mango and coconut
    ice-creams, 127
  Mango lassi, 61
maple syrup, 129
Matcha balls, 46–7
medjool dates, 32
  Cacao balls, 34–5
  Cashew balls, 37
  Chai-spiced sunflower
    seed balls, 38

Hemp seed balls, 44
Make it a date, 117
Matcha balls, 46–7
Oat balls, 36
time-saving tips, 22–3
Venus bar, 176–7
mesquite powder: Venus bar,
  176–7
midnight munchies
  Baked bananas, 106
  Brown rice, coconut oil
    and hemp seeds, 110
  Chocolate mousse, 103
  Coconut rice, 107
  Perfect parfait, 104
  Porridge three ways, 108–9
  Roasted veg frittata, 105
  Turmeric latte, 111
Mini baked potato, 157
mint
  Green pea dip (a.k.a. dippy),
    78
  Hit the tropics, 63
Mischel, Walter, 35
miso, 154
Mission Australia, 25–6
moods and food, 7–8,
  114–15
mousse: Chocolate mousse,
  103
muesli: Perfect parfait, 104

N

nutmeg, 38
nuts
  ABC nutter, 142
  Choconana, 59
  Honeyed walnuts, 183
  Matcha balls, 46–7
  Red pesto, 142
  Satay dip, 80
  Tamari nuts, 160–1
  time-saving tips, 21
  See also individual nuts

O

Oat balls, 36
oats (quick): Banana balls, 39
oats (rolled)
  Apricot balls, 41
  Banana oat bites (a.k.a.
    Bobs), 179
  Chocolate coconut balls, 48
  Oat balls, 36
  Porridge three ways, 108–9
  Smoosli, 56
obesity in young people, 9
oleic acid, 96
olives: Tapenade, 81
one bit wonders
  Boiled egg, 152–3
  Can of tomatoes, 159
  Chickpea pancake, 162
  Corn on the cob, 151
  Edamame, 150
  Fruit sticks, 156
  Haloumi/Saganaki, 155
  Mini baked potato, 157
  Roasted chickpeas, 158
  Salt and pepper coconut
    chips, 163
  Tamari nuts, 160–1
  Vegemite broth, 154

P

papaya: Hit the tropics, 63
Paper bag popcorn, 169
parsley: Gremolata, 141
parsnip: Beetroot, carrot and
  parsnip chips, 91
peanut butter: Satay dip, 80
pears: Tummy tonic, 64
peas: Green pea dip (a.k.a.
  dippy), 78
pepitas See pumpkin seeds
Perfect parfait, 104
phenols, 43
pine nuts: Green pea dip
  (a.k.a. dippy), 78
pineapples
  Hit the tropics, 63

I pine for you, 57
pistachios
    Matcha balls, 46–7
    Zucchini chips, 95
Polenta wedges, 93
polyphenols, 55, 135
poppy seeds, 37
Porridge three ways, 108–9
potatoes
    Mini baked potato, 157
    Salt and vinegar chips
        (sort of!), 96
production effect, 28
Prune and walnut balls
    (a.k.a. Prunut balls), 43
pumpkin seeds
    Almond butter bars, 178
    Desk mix, 170

Q

quercetin, 118
Quesadilla, 144

R

raspberries
    Fruitcicles, 128
    Raspberry chia, 58
    Up beet, 133
    Watermelon and raspberry
        icy poles, 126
red kidney beans: Quesadilla, 144
Red pesto, 142
rice
    Chinese pudding, 119
    Coconut rice, 107
    See also brown rice
ricotta
    Oat balls, 36
    Spinach and ricotta dip, 79
    Traffic light wrap, 143
rituals, creating family, 19, 171
Roasted chickpeas, 158
Roasted veg, 143
Roasted veg frittata, 105

S

Saganaki, 155
Salt and pepper coconut chips,
    163
Salt and vinegar chips (sort
    of!), 96
sandwiches
    ABC nutter, 142
    Apple sandwich, 118
    Avocado and. . . , 140
    Eggsellent, 141
    Fruit sandwich, 145
    Happy hummus, 144
    Quesadilla, 144
    Roasted veg, 143
    Say cheese. . . and Vegemite!
        140
    Smashed banana, 145
    Traffic light wrap, 143
Satay dip, 80
Say cheese. . . and Vegemite! 140
seeds
    nutritional value, 44, 49, 60
    time saving tips, 21
sesame seeds: Zesty coconut
    balls, 40
Simple guacamole, 73
sleep and effect on
    performance, 26
sleep deprivation, 101–2
Smashed banana, 145
Smoosli, 56
smoothies
    ABC, 54
    açaí, 55
    bulking up, 53
    Choconana, 59
    Hit the tropics, 63
    I pine for you, 57
    It's easy being green, 62
    Mango lassi, 61
    Raspberry chia, 58
    Smoosli, 56
    Zucchini and kefir, 60
snacking, tips for good, 13–15

soft drinks, sugar in, 18, 166
soups
    Can of tomatoes, 159
    Spinach soup, 119
    Vegemite broth, 154
soybeans: Edamame, 150
spinach (baby)
    I pine for you, 57
    It's easy being green, 62
    Kombucha 'juice,' 67
    Spinach and ricotta dip, 79
    Spinach soup, 119
spirulina, 54
spreads
    Gremolata, 141
    Red pesto, 142
Strawberry chia pots, 182
stress of study, 25–9
sugar
    consumption and
        alternatives, 166–8
    moods and, 8, 114
    processed, 10
    recommended, 18
sundried tomatoes, 105
    Red pesto, 142
sunflower seeds
    Almond butter bars, 178
    Chai-spiced sunflower
        seed balls, 38
Super Size Me, 88
Super-speedy egg, 120
Sweet Poison (Gillespie), 18
sweet potatoes
    Brownies, 180–1
    Sweet potato fries, 94
sweet things
    Almond butter bars, 178
    Banana oat bites (a.k.a.
        Bobs), 179
    Bountee bites, 174
    Brownies, 180–1
    Cheery ripes, 172–3
    Chocolate bark, 175
    Coconut crumbles, 171
    Desk mix, 170

Honeyed walnuts, 183
Paper bag popcorn, 169
Strawberry chia pots, 182
Venus bar, 176–7

T

tahini, 82
    Happy hummus, 144
    Hummus balls, 45
    Hummus in a hurry, 72
    Tahini balls, 49
Tamari nuts, 160–1
Tapenade, 81
That Sugar Film, 18
The Six Cs, 117
tiger nuts: Desk mix, 170
time-saving tips for food
   preparation, 19–24
tomatoes
    Can of tomatoes, 159
    Tomato salsa, 77
    Veggie poles, 132
Traffic light wrap, 143
trans fat, 148
tryptophan, 37, 60
Tummy tonic, 64
Turmeric latte, 111
Tzatziki, 75

U

Up beet, 133

V

Vegemite, 139
    Say cheese. . . and Vegemite!
    140
    Vegemite broth, 154
vegetables
    Blanched greens, 120
    Roasted veg frittata, 105
    The Six Cs, 117
    time-saving tips, 22
Veggie poles, 132
Venus bar, 176–7
vitamin A, 74, 82
vitamin B6, 106
vitamin D, 81
vitamin K, 60, 64, 104, 118, 172

W

walnuts
    Cacao balls, 34–5
    Desk mix, 170
    Gremolata, 141
    Honeyed walnuts, 183
    Make it a date, 117
    Oat balls, 36
    Prune and walnut balls
      (a.k.a. Prunut balls), 43
Watermelon and raspberry icy
   poles, 126

Y

yoghurt
    D.I.Y. yoghurt pot, 121
    Mango lassi, 61
    nutritional value, 56, 75
    Perfect parfait, 104
    Tzatziki, 75

Z

Zesty coconut balls, 40
zucchini
    Roasted veg frittata, 105
    Traffic light wrap, 143
    Zucchini and kefir, 60
    Zucchini chips, 95

SMART SNACKS

FLIP SHELTON is a mother who's passionate about good food and healthy food choices. For over 20 years she has inspired people about food on radio and TV, starting at Melbourne's 3RRR radio station and continuing with regular spots including *Good Morning Australia* and *Surprise Chef*, and countless cooking demonstrations. She has written for various magazines, newspapers and online publications, and ten years ago established her own muesli production business, Flip's Muesli. *Smart Snacks* is her third cookbook.

DR MICHAEL CARR-GREGG is one of Australia's highest profile adolescent and child psychologists. He has worked as an academic, researcher and political lobbyist, and is the author of 13 books. An ambassador for the Make-A-Wish Foundation, Smiling Mind and Big Brothers Big Sisters, he also sits on the board of the Family Peace Foundation and the National Centre Against Bullying. Michael is the resident parenting expert on Channel 7's *Sunrise* and the psychologist for Channel 9's *Morning Extra*, as well as the *Morning Show* with Neil Mitchell on Radio 3AW. He is married with two sons and is a special patron of the Hawthorn Football Club.